50 Common Errors

A Practical Guide for English Learners

Bob Marsden

Merriam-Webster, Incorporated
Springfield, Massachusetts, U.S.A.

Copyright © 2008 by Bob Marsden

ISBN: 978-087779-681-7

Library of Congress Cataloging-in-Publication Data

Marsden, Bob
    50 common errors : a practical guide for English learners / Bob Marsden.
        p. cm.
    Includes index.
    ISBN 978-0-87779-681-7
    1. English language—Textbooks for foreign speakers.   2. English
language—Errors in usage.   I. Title.   II. Title: Fifty common errors.
    PE1128.M3426 2008
    428.2'4—dc22

                                       2008033239

Made in the United States of America

5432 QW/V12111009

Contents

Preface   vi

        calves   *sheep*
1. The farmer has a lot of ~~calfs~~ but no ~~sheeps~~. (Plurals)   1

        is   *are*
2. The news ~~are~~ bad, and the people ~~is~~ worried. (Plural nouns)   4

        It's   *parents'*
3. ~~Its~~ my ~~parent's~~ car. (Apostrophes, possessives, contractions)   6

        English   *June*
4. I started learning ~~english~~ last ~~june~~. (Capital letters)   10

        a teacher   *a doctor*
5. Are you ~~teacher~~? No, I am ~~doctor~~. (Indefinite article: *a, an*)   13

        Life
6. ~~The life, it~~ is beautiful. (Definite article: *the*)   16

        any   *some*
7. I don't have ~~some~~ sugar but I have ~~any~~ milk. (*Some/any*, etc.)   21

        a lot of   *many*
8. He has ~~many~~ money but not ~~much~~ friends. (Count and noncount nouns, *many/much*)   24

        little   *few*
9. He has ~~few~~ money and ~~little~~ friends. (Count and noncount nouns, *few/little*)   27

        is   *are*
10. Each ~~are~~ unique, but all of them ~~is~~ good. (*All/every/each/whole/entire*)   29

        shorter
11. She is ~~more shorter~~ than her son. (Comparative)   32

        most modern   *in*
12. It's the ~~modernest~~ building ~~of~~ the city. (Superlative)   36

        big enough   *enough bedrooms*
13. Our house is ~~enough big~~ and it has ~~bedrooms enough~~. (*Enough, too*)   39

        such a
14. He is ~~a so~~ good friend. (*So/such*)   42

        well
15. He knows he can't write ~~good~~. (Adverbs)   44

        two-door
16. It's a ~~two doors~~ car. (Compound adjectives)   48

17. They lived in ~~a brick white old~~ house. (Adjective order) *an old white brick* 50

18. He ~~approached carefully~~ the building. (Adverb placement) *carefully approached* 53

19. ~~Do you can~~ meet me at the restaurant? (Modals) *Can you* 55

20. She ~~have~~ a brother who ~~live~~ in Mexico. (Third-person singular) *has* *lives* 57

21. You are ~~drive~~ too fast. (Present continuous, simple present) *driving* 59

22. I haven't ~~saw~~ him because he ~~haven't~~ come home yet. (Present perfect) *seen* *hasn't* 62

23. I haven't ~~gone~~ to Mali but I ~~have visited~~ Chad in 2006. (Simple past, present perfect) *been* *visited* 66

24. I ~~am~~ sitting here ~~since~~ two hours. (Present perfect continuous, *for, since*) *have been* *for* 69

25. By then, the guest of honor ~~left~~. (Past perfect) *had left* 72

26. The church has ~~offer~~ meals to homeless people. (Participles following auxiliaries) *offered* 74

27. It was the most ~~depressed~~ movie I've ever seen. (Participles as adjectives) *depressing* 76

28. I ~~was living~~ in France, but I left in 2002. (*Used to* as auxiliary) *used to live* 78

29. I will tell him when I ~~will see~~ him tomorrow. (Time clauses, *when*) *see* 82

30. We recommend that you ~~are~~ prepared. (Subjunctive) *be* 84

31. If I ~~would live~~ here, I would run every day. (Conditional sentences) *lived* 86

32. If she ~~would have~~ seen it, she would have told me. (Conditional sentences) *had* 90

33. She wishes you ~~live~~ nearer. *(Wish)* *lived* 93

34. ~~One speaks English~~ here. (Passive voice) *English is spoken* 97

35. When ~~begins the class~~? (Questions with auxiliaries) *does the class begin* 100

36. He ~~told~~ that he ~~is~~ hungry. (Reported statements, *tell/say*) *said* *was* 101

37. He asked where <u>~~is my mother~~</u>. (Reported questions)   *my mother was*   106

38. He told me <u>~~don't~~</u> do it. (Reported commands)   *not to*   109

39. I <u>~~want~~</u> speak English but I can't <u>~~to speak~~</u> English. (Infinitives with and without *to*)   *want to*   *speak*   113

40. She finished her paper and handed <u>~~in it~~</u>. (Phrasal verbs)   *it in*   115

41. I came here <u>~~for to~~</u> learn English. (Infinitive of purpose)   *to*   118

42. I still miss my <u>~~father that~~</u> I loved dearly. (Relative clauses)   *father, who*   120

43. Last night is the time <u>~~it happened then~~</u>. (Relative adverbs)   *when it happened*   123

44. He was right, <u>~~isn't it~~</u>? (Tag questions)   *wasn't he*   125

45. <u>~~There is~~</u> dark, but <u>~~it is~~</u> some stores that are still open. (*There is, It is,* etc.)   *It is*   *there are*   129

46. <u>~~The place where I work there~~</u> is one hour away. (Repetition of sentence elements)   *The place where I work*   132

47. I <u>~~cut my hair~~</u> at the hairdresser's on West Street. (*Have/get* (something done))   *have my hair cut*   134

48. You <u>~~mustn't~~</u> be so polite. (*Must, have to*)   *don't have to*   136

49. When I <u>~~go~~</u> to stay with you, I will <u>~~take~~</u> it. (*Come/go, bring/take*)   *come*   *bring*   139

50. I am used to <u>~~drive~~</u> on the right, not the left. (*Be used to, get used to*)   *driving*   141

Reference Section I: The Tenses of English   143

Reference Section II: Common Irregular Verbs   150

Index   153

Preface

This book attempts to illustrate and explain points of English usage by focusing on the errors most commonly made by non-native speakers. Its explanations address many of the most common English structures. These explanations have been kept as simple as possible, in the belief that clarity and usefulness are far more important than absolute thoroughness. Their purpose is to help you use English structures correctly in *most* situations, rather than risk confusing you by explaining every possible usage.

The book was mainly intended for individual self-study, but it may also be used effectively in the classroom. It was written mainly for upper-intermediate students of English, but should also be of interest to more advanced students and even to teachers of English. Though certain errors are made more often by learners from certain language backgrounds, most of the errors discussed here are made frequently by students from many different backgrounds, so almost any intermediate or advanced learner will be able to profit from it.

The book's units are mostly quite independent of each other; thus, the learner can begin reading almost anywhere. Each unit is devoted to a single type of error. These errors vary widely in importance and complexity; thus, some units will seem rather simple while others will be more demanding. To help ensure that the material is thoroughly learned, almost 1,000 exercises have been provided. The answers are given at the end of the book, following two reference sections: a description of the English verb tenses, and a list of the common irregular verbs.

We hope the student of English will want to keep this book within reach—to consult it whenever a specific grammatical problem arises, or to open it at random whenever he or she has a few minutes free and wants to master another small feature of the English language.

1 The farmer has a lot of ~~calfs~~ *calves* but no ~~sheeps~~. *sheep*

As you can see, both errors in this title sentence involve plurals.

To form the plurals of most nouns, you simply add -*s:*

> Smithtown has a hotel and only one restaurant, but Mooreville has two hotels and six restaurants.

However, the plurals of some nouns are formed differently. To form the plurals of nouns ending in -*ch*, -*s*, -*sh*, -*x*, or -*z*, you normally add -*es:*

> church → churches   box → boxes
> glass → glasses   waltz → waltzes
> dish → dishes

For a few common words ending in -*o*, you form the plural by adding -*es:*

> echo → echoes   potato → potatoes
> hero → heroes   tomato → tomatoes

But for most words ending in -*o*, you form the plural in the regular way:

> piano → pianos
> photo → photos
> zero → zeros

For words ending in consonant + *y*, you change the *y* to *i* and add -*es*. But for words ending in vowel + *y*, you just add -*s*.

> baby → babies
> story → stories
> boy → boys
> monkey → monkeys

For a few common words ending in -*f* or -*fe*, you form the plural by dropping the -*f* or -*fe* and adding -*ves:*

calf → calves	leaf → leaves	scarf → scarves	thief → thieves
half → halves	life → lives	self → selves	wife → wives
hoof → hooves	loaf → loaves	shelf → shelves	wolf → wolves
knife → knives			

But for most words ending in *-f* or *-fe*, you simply add *-s*:

    roof → roofs
    safe → safes

A few common nouns form their plural by a vowel change:

    foot → feet
    goose → geese
    man → men
    mouse → mice
    tooth → teeth
    woman → women

Notice also:

    child → children
    ox → oxen

A few animal names keep the same form in the plural:

    deer → deer
    fish → fish
    sheep → sheep
    salmon → salmon

But most have regular plurals:

    bird → birds
    cow → cows
    eagle → eagles
    hen → hens
    rabbit → rabbits

Finally, a few common words from Greek and Latin still have their Greek and Latin plurals, even though they've been in the English language for a very long time:

1: The farmer has a lot of ~~calfs~~ *calves* but no ~~sheeps~~ *sheep*.

crisis → crises
analysis → analyses
fungus → fungi
alumnus → alumni
phenomenon → phenomena
larva → larvae

✓ Check —————————————————

1. Can You Remember?

Write the plurals of these nouns.

1. hotel _____
2. calf _____
3. monkey _____
4. echo _____
5. roof _____

6. zero _____
7. house _____
8. child _____
9. cow _____
10. sheep _____

2. Fill in the Blanks

Fill in each blank with the plural form of one of the nouns at the right.

1. Chicken soup is one of my favorite _____.	thief
2. We heard the _____ howling at the moon.	knife, fork
3. Most of the _____ in this town have red _____.	house, roof
4. I have autographs from all my soccer _____.	dish
5. We drove by three _____.	hero
6. A flock of _____ rested by the pond.	goose
7. No one saw the _____ leave the house.	wolf
8. Remember to put the _____ and _____ by the plates.	deer, baby
9. She's terrified of _____ and _____.	rat, mouse
10. I saw the _____ and their _____ at the park!	church

3. Rewrite the Sentences

Write new sentences, changing each noun from singular to plural.

Example: He wrote a good analysis of the problem.
→ He wrote good analyses of the problems.

1. There is a deer in the field. _____

2. The store had a piano in its window. _____

3. Please put the glass on the shelf. _____

4. The woman knows the man. _____

5. The baby already has a tooth. _____

6. She showed me a photo of a sheep. _____

7. Let's read the story about the rabbit. _____

8. The girl is buying a scarf. _____

9. Let the child eat it. _____

10. The tomato is in the bag, but the potato is in the box. _____

_____

2 The news ~~are~~ *is* bad, and the people ~~is~~ *are* worried.

The title sentence contains two nouns. One is singular, though it ends in *-s;* the other is plural, though it doesn't end in *-s.*

News is a noncount noun (like *soccer, fun, oxygen, machinery, flu, information, clothing, furniture, weather, air,* and *research*). Thus, you can say:

a little news
some news
not much news
a news item
a piece of news
a bit of news

2: The news ~~are~~ ^{is} bad, and the people ~~is~~ ^{are} worried.

but not:

> a news
> two news
> many news

A number of noncount nouns look like plurals but are usually treated as singular:

> Economics is his favorite subject.
> Measles infects millions of children every year.
> Politics doesn't [*or* don't] interest me.
> Classics includes the study of Greek and Latin.
> Physics isn't as popular as chemistry.

Some objects that have two main physical parts (mostly clothing and tools) have no singular form and are treated as plural:

> My pajamas aren't as old as they look.
> The shorts that she's wearing today are blue.
> His trousers weren't expensive, but they're very stylish.
> These glasses are the ones I use for reading.
> These scissors are sharp.
> I couldn't see anything through those binoculars.
> There are some pliers in the toolbox.

But notice that the phrase "a pair of . . ." is singular:

> That's a nice pair of pajamas.
> There's a pair of scissors on the table.
> She has a new pair of glasses, but they're not very attractive.

Count and noncount nouns are discussed again in Units 8 and 9.

✓ Check ─────────────

Choose the Correct Alternative

Underline the correct word from each pair, as in the example.

Example: This/These trousers is/<u>are</u> mine.

1. That/Those glasses suit/suits you.

2. The news was/were bad. It/They upset him very much.

3. This/These pajamas is/are nice, and it/they is/are comfortable too.

4. All this/these furniture is/are beautiful, and it/they is/are all for sale.

5. That/Those scissors is/are dull; it/they need/needs sharpening.

6. The information/informations that you need is/are in this envelope.

7. My shorts is/are old but I still like it/them.

8. This is an interesting research/piece of research.

9. Economics is/are based on mathematics.

10. Physics was/were Einstein's field of study.

3   It's   parents'
~~Its~~ my ~~parent~~'s car.

Using apostrophes is simple, but you can still see apostrophe mistakes on English signs all over the world—including the U.S. and Britain!

The apostrophe has two main uses: (1) to show the omission of letters, and (2) to show possession.

Apostrophes show the omission of letters mostly in contractions of auxiliary verbs and the adverb *not.* Notice that *-'s* can stand for *has* or *is,* and that *-'d* can stand for *had* or *would.*

am → -'m	has → -'s	will → -'ll
is → -'s	have → -'ve	would → -'d
are → -'re	had → -'d	not → -n't

We've been calling him for hours, but he hasn't been answering.
She's [=she has] already been to Australia three times, and she's [=she is] happy to be going back.

7

It's parents'

3: Its my parent's car.

He said he'd [=he had] met Angela once, so he'd [=he would] recognize her if he saw her again.

Most of the auxiliaries combine with *-n't.* However, *am* does not, *might, shall,* and *ought* rarely do, and *may* almost never does. *Won't* (will not) and *shan't* (shall not) are the only irregular examples.

isn't
aren't
wasn't
weren't
don't
doesn't
didn't
won't
wouldn't
haven't
hadn't
mustn't
can't
couldn't
shouldn't
mightn't
shan't
oughtn't
mayn't

(Note that *shan't* and *mayn't* are quite rare.)

Apostrophes are sometimes used to show omissions in other words, especially when imitating informal speech:

The station plays rock 'n' [=and] roll from the 1950s.
He told them he was in Hawaii, "ridin' [=riding] the waves and lovin' [=loving] every minute of it."

You use an apostrophe to show numbers omitted in dates:

I first met her in '68 [=1968] when she was a student.

A few old phrases contain an apostrophe; the most important is *o'clock* (which once was a quick way of saying "of the clock"):

> Meet me at the station at one o'clock.

In writing from earlier centuries, you will see many apostrophes for omitted letters:

> I was the owl that shriek'd [=shrieked], the fatal bellman,
> Which gives the stern'st [=sternest] good-night.
> (Shakespeare, *Macbeth*)

The second major use of the apostrophe is for showing possession or ownership. You add -'*s* to the end of singular nouns to show possession or ownership:

> John's Honda is light blue.
> The boy's coat is over there.
> Where is the dog's bowl?

You also add -'*s* to the end of the few irregular plurals that don't end in -*s*:

> The children's bedrooms are upstairs.
> Mike should be on the men's team, not the women's team!

For plural nouns ending in -*s*, you indicate possession by adding an apostrophe *after* the -*s*:

> My parents' car is in the garage.
> All the girls' bedrooms are upstairs.
> Here are both dogs' bowls.

It's always means either "it is" or "it has." To show possession, use *its* (with no apostrophe):

> It's [=It is] snowing now; in fact, it's [=it has] been snowing for hours.
> Each dog has its own bowl.

If a name ends in -*s*, some people indicate possession by simply adding an apostrophe; others add -'*s*:

> This is Charles' [*or* Charles's] coat, and that's James' [*or* James's] hat.

The apostrophe is also sometimes used to show certain plurals: the plurals of letters, numbers, quoted words, dates, and nouns that consist of initials:

There are two *l*'s in *hill*.
She remembered that his phone number had four 2's.
The first paragraph contained five *often*'s.
Most of us preferred the fashions of the 1960's [*or* 1960s] to those of the 1970's [*or* 1970s].
They bought six CD's [*or* CDs] and two DVD's [*or* DVDs].

Finally, many surnames of Irish origin start with *O'*:

He brought along two friends, Pat O'Neill and Michael O'Grady.

✓ Check

1. Add Apostrophes

Add apostrophes where necessary in the following sentences:

1. He isnt at home and we havent seen him for weeks.

2. She doesnt know where theyre hiding.

3. Im sure shes telling the truth, but Ill ask her again.

4. He said hed met Angela once before.

5. This is Johns car.

6. That is the boys coat.

7. Thats the dogs bowl.

8. Those are my childrens beds.

9. He should be on the mens team!

10. This is my parents car.

11. Those are the boys bedrooms.

12. Its been snowing for hours.

13. Each dog has its own bowl.

14. Every language has its own difficulties.

15. He is coming in two weeks time.

16. Id like a dollars worth of nails please.

17. Meet me at the station at one oclock.

18. There are two *l*s in *hill.*

19. Heres a list of dos and donts.

20. She grew up during the 60s.

2. Fix the Punctuation

Correct the apostrophes in the following sentences:

1. Sh'es not at work and she has'nt been there for week's.

2. Those are the childrens' book's.

3. He bought twenty dollar's worth of nail's.

4. Is it six 'oclock yet?

5. You mus'tnt drive Davids' car.

6. Thats' my childs' toy.

7. The girls' name is Charlotte Brown.

8. Each house has it's own mailbox.

9. These are my sister's bedrooms.

10. You must give two week's notice if your'e going to leave your job.

4 I started learning ~~english~~ *English* last ~~june~~ *June*.

Capital letters are mainly used for two purposes in English: (1) the beginnings of sentences, and (2) proper nouns and adjectives.

A capital letter is used for the first letter in a sentence or direct quotation:

The teacher came in and said quietly, "Open your books to page 48."

Capital letters are also often used for the beginning of each line of a poem or song:

The naming of cats is a difficult matter,
It isn't just one of your holiday games;
You may think at first I'm as mad as a hatter
When I tell you a cat must have three different names.
(T. S. Eliot, "The Naming of Cats")

They are also used for proper nouns. Proper nouns include:

- Names of people and their initials:

   I was lucky enough to meet Bill Clinton and George W. Bush.

- People's titles, when they are used as part of a name:

   I was amazed to see Mr. and Mrs. Smith, the dead man's neighbors.
   The heads of state included Queen Elizabeth and President Sarkozy.

- Names of days of the week, festivals and holidays, and months:

   I'm meeting Carl next Monday, which is Memorial Day.
   Is it true that Christmas Day is always December 25th?

- Names of countries, peoples, and their languages:

   The people of Switzerland are called the Swiss. They speak French, German,
   and Italian.

- Place-names and geographical features:

   His address is Seaview Cottage, 3 Church Street, Stoke Newington, Devon,
   England.
   I especially wanted to see Mount Rushmore and Death Valley, but many
   tourists prefer the Grand Canyon or the Mississippi River.

- Names of books, newspapers, films, plays, stories, works of art, etc.:

   The movie *Apocalypse Now* was based on Conrad's novel *Heart of Darkness*.
   There's a good article in the *New York Times* about Mozart's *Requiem.*

- Names of religions:

   The world's largest religions are Christianity, Islam, Hinduism, and
   Buddhism.

- Names of organizations, including initials:

    The U.S. Department of Education has met with Microsoft to discuss
        computers in the classroom.
    There was a good program on the BBC about the American CIA.

- Names of historical periods and events:

    Did he fight in the American Revolution or the War of 1812?
    My history course covers the centuries between the Renaissance and the
        French Revolution.

- Brand names:

    He drives a Ford and drinks Guinness.

Capital letters are also used for *proper adjectives* (adjectives based on proper nouns):

    These are my Brazilian friends.
    It's one of the largest Buddhist temples.
    The Elizabethan era was a glorious time for England.
    His brother is a Marine colonel.

✓ Check

Provide Capitals

Put capital letters in the right places in the following sentences.

1. she came in and said, "we will be taking a short quiz this morning."

2. i was standing near bill clinton during the press conference.

3. queen elizabeth and president sarkozy were invited to the event at the un.

4. i was happy to see my neighbor, ms. jones.

5. we open our presents on christmas day, not christmas eve.

6. i'm meeting john next monday.

7. the people of canada are the canadians; they speak english and french.

8. my address is 100 commonwealth ave., boston, massachusetts.

9. we drove through death valley on our way to see the grand canyon.

10. she converted from catholicism to buddhism.

11. the u.s. department of defense is seeking more funding from congress.

12. did he fight in world war I or world war II?

13. she prefers to drink stolichnaya when she can get it.

14. the movie *clueless* was based on jane austen's novel *emma*.

15. there is a long article in the sunday *new york times* about beethoven and his works.

5   *a teacher*   *a doctor*
Are you ~~teacher~~? - No, I am ~~doctor~~.

A (or *an*), which is known as the *indefinite article*, has many uses. Some are different from the uses of the indefinite article in other languages. (And some languages have no articles at all!) In many languages, the indefinite article isn't used when you state a person's **profession, but in English it is required, as shown in the title sentence.**

Normally *a* is used before a consonant, and *an* before a vowel:

> It's a horse. / It's an elephant.
> She wears a yellow dress every day. / She wears an orange dress every day.

But the actual rule is that *a* is used before a consonant *sound* and *an* before a vowel *sound*. In the sentences below, the words after *a* begin with a *y-* sound, and the words after *an* begin with vowel sounds:

> She wears a uniform for her job.
> It's a European car.
> This car can go 140 miles an hour.
> They showed me an X-ray of my knee.

A (an) is used only before singular count nouns. It is used:

- Before a noun that names something for the first time:

> She noticed a strange animal moving across the field.
> They stopped a man to ask where the store was.
> A new problem had emerged.

- Before a noun that represents a general example:

    She's still only a girl.
    My mother was a lawyer.
    I'd like an orange, please.
    Has he found a job yet?
    He's a cousin of mine.
    You can't cut a rock with scissors.
    A professor usually teaches for only eight or nine months each year.
    It was a gloomy day.

- Like the word *one* in many phrases naming amounts or quantities:

    a hundred
    a thousand
    a lot of
    a few
    a little
    a third of the size
    a week

- In place of *per* in phrases involving price, speed, time, etc.:

    These apples cost ninety cents a pound.
    He was driving at 30 miles an hour.
    Twice a week the nurse comes to see her.

- After *what* and *such* before a noun phrase:

    What a beautiful painting!
    She was such a happy person.

The definite article, *the*, is discussed in Unit 6.

✔ Check

1. Can You Remember?

Fill in each blank with *a* or *an*.

1. She is ___ good friend.

2. She is ___ teacher.

3. He is ___ engineer.

4. It's ___ elephant.

5. This car can go 140 miles ___ hour.

6. This is ___ X-ray.

7. John is ___ cabdriver.

8. It's ___ European car.

9. What ___ beautiful painting!

10. I bought ___ orange and some bread.

2. *A, An,* or no article?

Fill in each blank with *a, an,* or Ø (meaning "no article").

1. Jane Walker is ___ nurse.

2. She wears ___ uniform to work.

3. It takes her ___ hour to drive to work.

4. Her car is ___ MG, which is ___ European car.

5. Jane has two children: ___ two-year-old boy and ___ eleven-year-old girl.

6. She's such ___ busy woman!

7. For Jane the most important things in ___ life are ___ health and ___ happiness.

8. Jane's husband, John, is ___ engineer.

9. He just bought ___ hundred nails at twenty cents ___ dozen.

10. John's parents are both ___ teachers.

11. John thinks that Jane is ___ good mother and ___ good wife.

12. Jane thinks that John is ___ good father and ___ good husband.

6 The ~~life~~ Life, it is beautiful.

Like the indefinite article (see Unit 5), the *definite article, the*, has many uses. Some of them are different from the uses of the definite article in other languages (if those languages even have articles). Many languages use the definite article with all abstract nouns, such as *life* in the title sentence; in English, however, abstract nouns usually don't take an article.

Here are more examples of abstract nouns with no article:

> She's still looking for love.
> Wealth doesn't always bring happiness.
> They want freedom, but they also want security.

But when a noun that is normally abstract is used more specifically, *the* is used:

> All he needed was the love of a good woman.
> The total wealth of the family was about $5 million.
> They now enjoyed the freedom to travel abroad.

The is also used:

- Before nouns that refer to things or people that are common in daily life or that occur in nature:

> She's on the phone with her husband right now.
> Ask the librarian for help.
> What time does the mail come?
> There was a bright light in the sky.

- Before a noun that refers to a person or thing that has already been mentioned or is clearly understood from the context or situation:

> We stopped in front of a small house. The house looked empty.
> George is in the kitchen. [=the kitchen of this house/apartment]
> Pass the potatoes, please. [=the potatoes on the table]
> Can I see the book you're reading? Who is the author?

- Before the names of specific organizations, places, events, works of art, etc.:

> The CIA and the FBI were working together.
> It lies very near the equator.
> He plays for the Boston Red Sox.
> Have you been to the Louvre? Did you see the *Mona Lisa?*

- Before singular nouns that refer in a general way to people or things of a specified kind:

  > The raccoon is native to North America.
  > These training videos will be useful to both the novice and the expert.

- Before plural nouns that refer to every person or thing of a specified kind:

  > It's a tradition practiced by the Japanese.

- Before the plural form of a person's last name, to show that all the members of the family are included:

  > The Browns are coming here for dinner Friday.

- Before nouns that refer to a particular unit or period of time:

  > She's not here at the moment.
  > There was a great deal of social unrest in the 1960s.

- Before superlatives and *first, second,* etc.:

  > It's the highest building in the city.
  > We dined at the best restaurant in San Francisco.
  > Your room is on the third floor.

- Before nouns that refer in a general way to a specific type of activity:

  > She works in the publishing industry.
  > Do you know how to dance the waltz?

- Before the names of island groups, mountain ranges, seas and oceans, rivers, and plural names of countries:

  > She lives in the Azores.
  > His plane crashed in the Andes.
  > Elat is a port on the Red Sea.
  > The Colorado River is one of the longest in the U.S.
  > Amsterdam is the capital of the Netherlands.

- Before a person's title:

  We met the Secretary-General of the United Nations.
  Write a letter to the president of the company.
  The movie is about the Queen of England.

The is not used:

- Before names of people, including names with titles:

  Professor Lawton handed back the exams.
  The movie is about Queen Elizabeth.

- Before the names of towns and cities, streets, and most countries:

  Mrs. O'Hara sold her house in Ireland and bought a new one on Fearing
    Street in Glasgow.

- Before indefinite plural nouns:

  Horses like carrots, and rabbits like lettuce.

- Before nouns that refer to most diseases and subjects of study:

  In college he studied economics.
  She has been diagnosed with cancer.
  Two of his aunts had diabetes.

- Before the word *home* and nouns that refer to meals:

  I'm going home and I'll be staying home tonight.
  They were eating dinner when she arrived.

- Before nouns that refer to established organizations and common practices and
  activities:

  They always went to bed at 10:00.
  The family goes to church every Sunday.
  They finally took their neighbors to court.
  He's been in prison for five years.
  Their daughters are still in school.
  My husband was at work that day.

Notice that when these words are used to refer to a particular building, location, etc., that is used for the activities of the organization rather than to the organization itself, *the* is used:

> They do volunteer work at the local Catholic church on Wednesdays.
> Every month she traveled 300 miles to the prison to see her son.

The is usually pronounced "thuh" before a consonant sound, but "thee" before a vowel sound. (Remember that a vowel sound is sometimes spelled with a consonant, as in "honest" and "NFL," and a consonant sound is sometimes spelled with a vowel, as in "universe" and "euro.")

> I prefer the [pronounced "thuh"] French anthem to the ["thee"] American anthem.
> He didn't like the ["thee"] ending of the ["thuh"] movie.
> What's the ["thee"] honest thing to do?
> The ["thee"] NFL is America's professional football league.
> The ["thuh"] universe is full of mysteries.
> Britain uses the ["thuh"] pound, but Ireland uses the ["thuh"] euro.

The title sentence includes another English error: the use of "it" after "The life." Some languages let you emphasize a noun by following it with a pronoun that stands for the same noun ("This car, it is absolutely magnificent"), but in English this is never done.

✓ Check ———————————————————

1. *The*, *A*, or *An*?

Fill in each blank with *the*, *a*, or *an*.

1. This problem is important, but it's not _____ matter of life and death.

2. He never got over _____ death of his father.

3. There was _____ bright light in _____ sky.

4. George is in _____ garage.

5. At _____ end of _____ road, there was _____ house. _____ house looked empty.

6. That is _____ man who took my bag.

7. _____ Mississippi is _____ longest river in _____ U.S.

8. Amsterdam is _____ biggest city in _____ Netherlands.

9. We go to _____ local grocery store, but I like _____ store in _____ city much better.

10. His wife has been in _____ hospital for _____ last three weeks.

2. *The* or no article?

Fill in the blanks with *the* or Ø ("no article").

1. I think that _____ most important things in _____ life are _____ health and happiness.

2. George never recovered from _____ loss of his business.

3. I have a red rose, a white rose, and a pink rose, but _____ red rose is _____ prettiest one.

4. That is _____ largest business in _____ city.

5. Amundsen was _____ first man to reach _____ South Pole.

6. Henry is in _____ garden and Lucy is in _____ bathroom.

7. _____ telephone is over there, on _____ television and next to _____ lamp.

8. _____ man in _____ black hat can give you all _____ information that you need.

9. _____ Rockies are not near _____ New York; they are closer to _____ West Coast of the U.S.

10. _____ Seychelles are a group of islands in _____ Indian Ocean.

11. _____ Thames is _____ most famous river in _____ England.

12. I know that _____ bears hibernate, and I think that _____ hedgehogs hibernate, too.

13. He leaves _____ home at 7:00 in _____ morning, and he gets back to _____ house at 7:00 in _____ evening.

14. When they lived in _____ U.S., they went to _____ church every Sunday.

15. He has four children: three girls and a boy. _____ oldest girl is in _____ college, and _____ youngest girl is in _____ school in _____ Switzerland.

7 I don't have ~~some~~ *any* sugar but I have ~~any~~ *some* milk.

The basic rule for using the adjectives *any* and *some* is: Use *some* in positive statements; use *any* in negative statements.

> There's some cream, but there aren't any eggs.
> There are some good bars in this town, but there aren't any good restaurants.

However, *some* is often used in negative sentences when it refers to something or someone not named or identified specifically. And *any* is often used in positive statements when it means "whichever" or "one or another."

> I don't like some of your friends.
> Any French movie would be fine with me.

In questions for which the answer is "yes" or "no," *any* is more common than *some*, but both are used. *Some* is usually used when the speaker expects the answer to be "yes."

> Is there any [*or* some] fruit in the kitchen?
> Are there any [*or* some] movie theaters near your apartment?

Somewhere, something, sometime, some more, someone, and *somebody* are generally used like *some*—that is, in positive statements:

> He lives somewhere in Europe.
> I'm looking for somebody to help me.
> I want to buy her something special.
> There was some more discussion, and then we all went home.

But *something, someone,* and *somebody* occasionally appear in negative statements:

> Something isn't right.
> Someone wasn't paying attention.

Anywhere, anything, anytime, any more, anyone, and *anybody* are often used like *any*—that is, mostly in negative statements—but they are fairly common in positive statements as well.

> I don't have anywhere to stay.
> Was there any more discussion of the subject?

My parents don't want anything for Christmas.
We can meet anytime you want.

In a negative answer to an *any* question, the opposite of *any* is *no* (or *not any*):

Are there any spoons? There are no spoons [=There aren't any spoons], but there are some forks.

✔ Check

1. Fill in the Blanks

Fill in the blanks with *some, any, somewhere, something, someone, somebody, anywhere, anything, anyone,* **or** *anybody.*

1. There isn't _____ in the fridge to eat.

2. I would like _____ fruit, please.

3. I want to eat _____ hot.

4. I'm not going _____ today.

5. Do you have _____ questions?

6. I lost the key _____ in the house.

7. Is _____ coming to our party? If not, we'll have to cancel it.

8. You're very pale. Is _____ wrong?

9. We spoke to _____ who looked like your brother.

10. I can't find _____ shoes that I like.

2. Make Sentences

Use the following words with *some* **or** *any* **to make sentences like the example sentence below. Make a positive statement about a word with a check mark (✔), and a negative statement about a word with an ✗.**

Example: spaghetti (✔)   sauce (✗)
          I'd like some spaghetti, but I don't want any sauce.

1. wine (✔)   cheese (✗)

7: I don't have ~~some~~ *any* sugar but I have ~~any~~ *some* milk.

2. rice (✗)   salad (✓)

   _____

3. bread (✓)   butter (✗)

   _____

4. ham (✓)   mustard (✗)

   _____

5. peas (✗)   potatoes (✓)

   _____

3. Questions and Answers

Write an answer sentence for each question below, using *some* or *any*. Make a positive statement about a word followed by a check mark (✓), and a negative statement about a word followed by an ✗. Remember the rules regarding negative answers to questions with *any*.

Example: Is there any beer or wine in the cabinet? wine (✓) beer (✗)
   - There's some wine in the cabinet, but there isn't any beer. *or*
   - There's some wine in the cabinet, but there's no beer.

1. Do you need some coffee or tea?   coffee (✓) tea (✗)

   _____

2. Are there any museums or art galleries in this city?   museums (✓) art galleries (✗)

   _____

3. Do we have any jam or peanut butter?   jam (✓) peanut butter (✗)

   _____

4. Are there any restaurants or bars in this town?   restaurants (✗) bars (✓)

   _____

5. Are there any herbs or spices in this dish?   herbs (✓) spices (✗)

   _____

6. Is there any ginger or garlic in this dish?   ginger (✗) garlic (✓)

   _____

7. Do you need some brownies or cookies?   brownies (✗) cookies (✓)

---

8. Is there any milk or orange juice in the fridge?   milk (✗) orange juice (✓)

---

9. Do we have some string or wire in the shed?   string (✓) wire (✗)

---

10. Are there any Mexicans or Brazilians in the school?   Mexicans (✓) Brazilians (✗)

---

8 He has ~~many~~ *a lot of* money but not ~~much~~ *many* friends.

Nouns in English can be divided into two main types: *count nouns* and *noncount nouns*. Count nouns refer to people or things that can be counted and that have both a singular and a plural form:

> I bought a red pepper and two small green peppers.
> The Arctic Ocean is one of only four oceans.
> He hunted among the children for his own child.

Noncount nouns refer to something that can't be counted individually; thus, they are always singular:

> Plants need heat and light.
> Money is nice, but it can't buy love.
> We'll need some rice and a pint of milk.

Notice that *pint* is a count noun but *milk* is noncount.

Many is used with count nouns; *much* is used with noncount nouns:

> How many potatoes should I buy?
> How much rice do they produce?

8: He has ~~many~~ *a lot of* money but not ~~much~~ *many* friends.

There aren't many children in the playground.
I don't have much time to talk right now.

Notice that two of the four sentences above are negative, and the other two only use *much* and *many* in the question phrases "How much" and "How many." In positive statements, *a lot (of)*, *lots (of)*, and *plenty (of)* are more common than *much* or *many*:

We have lots of potatoes.
They eat a lot of rice.
How many bottles of wine do we have? – A lot.
How much juice is there? – Plenty.

✓ Check ———————————————————

1. Write Conversations

For each exercise, write a question and two answers. Use the first answer to say that you do not have a lot of the named thing; use the other to say that you have a lot of it.

Examples: sugar   How much sugar is there?
- Not much. - There is plenty of / a lot of sugar.

banana   How many bananas are there?
- Not many. - There are plenty of / a lot of bananas.

1. coffee   _____

_____

_____

2. tomato   _____

_____

_____

3. man   _____

_____

_____

4. water _____

_____

_____

5. flour _____

_____

_____

2. Provide Answers

The Jones family is going shopping. Mr. Jones is in the kitchen, seeing what food and drink they have. Mrs. Jones asks questions from the dining room. Use the cues below to answer Mrs. Jones's questions. State that you have more of the first thing, and less of the second thing listed.

Example:　　　coffee, tea　　　How much tea is there?
　　　　　　　　　　　　　　There isn't much tea, but there's a lot of coffee.

1. pears, apples　　　How many apples are there?

_____

2. beef, pork　　　How much beef do we have?

_____

3. beans, peas　　　How many peas are there?

_____

4. pasta, rice　　　How much pasta is there?

_____

5. potatoes, beets　　　How many potatoes do we have?

_____

27

9: He has ~~few~~ *little* money and ~~little~~ *few* friends.

9 He has ~~few~~ *little* money and ~~little~~ *few* friends.

In Unit 8 we discussed using *many* with count nouns and *much* with noncount nouns. In the same way, *few* and *a few* are used with count nouns, and *little* and *a little* with non-count nouns:

> Few countries are bigger than Brazil.
> There are only a few trees in the park.
> The plan has little hope of success.
> All we need is a little luck.

The comparative form of *few* is *fewer*. (You cannot say "a fewer.")

> There are fewer mountains in Denmark than in Norway.
> We have fewer girls in our class than you have in yours.

The comparative form of *little* is *less*. (You cannot say "a less" except before an adjective.)

> Americans drink less wine than the French do.
> Try giving the plant less water.

However, *less* is commonly used with count nouns that refer to distances and amounts of money:

> It's less than 3 miles to town.
> The system is available at a cost of less than $5,000.

It's also used in mathematical expressions and in certain phrases:

> It's an angle of less than 60 degrees.
> Write an essay of 500 words or less.

Less is also sometimes used with other plural nouns, but many people consider such uses incorrect. Native speakers never confuse *few* and *little*.

A few and *a little* usually sound more positive than *few* and *little*:

> There are few good Chinese restaurants in the city, but there's a good Japanese place.

  There are a few good Chinese restaurants in the city, so we'll have a choice.
  There's little work left to do, so you can go home.
  Could you stay? There's a little work still left to do.

Quite a few means "many":

  Happy people usually have quite a few friends.

The superlative form of *little* is *the least,* and the superlative form of *few* is *the fewest*:

  He always does whatever requires the least effort.
  This car has had the fewest problems of any car we've ever owned.

✓ Check ———————————————————————

1. Can You Remember?

Answer the questions using *a little* **or** *a few.*

Examples: Is there any coffee? Yes, there is a little.
      Are there any apples? Yes, there are a few.

 1. Is there any tea? _____

 2. Are there any tomatoes? _____

 3. Are there any children in the playground? _____

 4. Do we have any wine? _____

 5. Is there any rice left? _____

2. Fill in the Blanks

Fill in the blank in each sentence with *few, fewer, little,* **or** *less.*

 1. I have _____ hope that he will be found.

 2. There are _____ farms in the area than there were when I was young.

 3. You'll find a gas station _____ than two miles from here.

 4. _____ women have achieved as much as she has.

 5. Please give your answer in 50 words or _____.

 6. We've had _____ rain this spring than last spring.

29

10: Each ~~are~~ ^{is} unique, but all of them ~~is~~ ^{are} good.

7. There are _____ good restaurants in this town now.

8. I got a rental car, but I had _____ luck finding a hotel room.

9. There are a _____ good places to eat in town.

10. He had a _____ job offers to choose from.

10 Each ~~are~~ ^{is} unique, but all of them ~~is~~ ^{are} good.

There are several different ways of saying "all":

> All [of] the students in the class are under 18.
> Every student in the class is under 18.
> Each student in the class is under 18.
> The whole class is under 18.
> The entire class is under 18.

Let's look at the five words used here: *all (of)*, *every*, *each*, *whole*, and *entire*.

All (of) can be used more broadly than the other four words. It can be used with both count and noncount nouns, and with both singular and plural nouns. It can also be followed by both singular and plural verb forms.

> All [of] the streets in this part of town are narrow.
> All of the street has been closed to traffic.
> All [of] the food is in that bag.
> All [of] the apples are ripe.

Every can only be used with count nouns and always takes a singular verb form:

> Every country has an embassy in Washington.
> Every one of our employees is important to the company's success.

Each, like *every*, can only be used with count nouns and always takes a singular verb form, but *each* emphasizes the individual:

> We carefully considered each proposal.

Each of our three sons has a different attitude to life.
The gifts were perfect, since each had been carefully chosen.

Notice that *each* is used as a pronoun in the last two sentences. However, *every* can never be used as a pronoun; thus, you could not say "Every of our three sons . . ." or "Every had been . . ."

Whole and *entire* are mostly used with singular nouns, but not always:

The whole [*or* entire] idea was ridiculous.
His entire [*or* whole] body is covered in tattoos.
They made us wait for three whole [*or* entire] hours.

When talking about only two things, you must use *both* rather than *all (of) the*:

Both of the twins are very tall, but all of the other children are of average height.

To refer to two things individually, you use *each* rather than *every*:

Their uncle gave $50 to each of the twins [*or* to each twin].

✓ Check ─────────────────────────────────────

1. Fill in the Blanks

Fill in the blanks with *all, each, every, whole, entire,* **or** *both.*

1. _____ the drivers are over 21.

2. _____ driver is over 21.

3. The _____ class is under 18.

4. _____ the streets in this part of town are closed.

5. The _____ store is under construction.

6. _____ state in the U.S. has two senators.

7. We reviewed _____ individual application very carefully.

8. _____ the food is in that bag.

9. _____ one of our family members is important to us.

10. _____ piece of china had been carefully chosen.

1: Each are *is* unique, but all of them is *are* good.

11. His _____ hand was burned.

12. _____ the twins are good at basketball.

13. I gave candy to _____ of the three boys.

14. _____ of our four children want to go into medicine.

15. The movie lasted three _____ hours!

2. Rewrite

Rewrite these sentences so that they begin with the word given.

1. All the books in this shop are on sale.

   Every _____

2. Every person in this town has the right to vote.

   All _____

3. All (of) the family is invited.

   The whole _____

4. All the chairs need to be replaced.

   Every _____

5. Each house on this street is different.

   All _____

6. All the bottles have been recycled.

   Every _____

7. Both of his parents are very intelligent.

   Each _____

8. Her whole leg is covered in mosquito bites.

   All of _____

9. All the teams in the competition are European.

   Every _____

10. Every plant in the garden needs water.

    All _____

11 She is <u>more ~~shorter~~</u> than her son.

(shorter written above "more shorter")

The sentence above shows an error in the comparative form of an adjective.

The comparative of short (one-syllable) adjectives is almost always formed by adding *-er* (or just *-r* if the adjective ends in *-e*):

> Her second novel is longer than her first one.
> Jack is tall, but his brother is taller.
> They were all nicer back then.

The comparative of longer adjectives is formed by using *more* or *less*:

> I think that pink roses are more beautiful than red ones.
> He found Los Angeles less interesting than San Francisco.
> Life is more difficult now.

As the title sentence shows, *more* (or *less*) and the *-er* form are never used for an adjective at the same time.

Notice that *than* is always used before the second thing being compared. Sometimes, however, the second thing isn't actually stated because it has already been stated or is obvious:

> Life is more difficult now.
> The neighbors have been less noisy recently.

When a one-syllable adjective ends with a consonant following a single vowel, you double the consonant before adding *-er*: *thin → thinner; sad → sadder;* etc.:

> Tim is fat, but his brother Paul is even fatter.

A few common adjectives have irregular comparatives:

bad → worse	many → more
far → farther *or* further	much → more
good → better	well → better
little → less	

It's a good movie, but the other one's better.
That song is really bad, much worse than I had remembered.

Most two-syllable adjectives form the comparative with *more* or *less*. These include all two-syllable adjectives that end in *-ed, -ful, -ing,* and *-less.*

She's more concerned about the problem than I am.
They'll be more careful this time.

But some two-syllable adjectives, including most adjectives that end in *-y*, generally take *-er*, with the *-y* changing to *i*.

No streets could be dustier than these are in the dry season.
Their garden has never been prettier.

And some may take either *more* or *-er:*

That's the more simple [*or* simpler] and more common [*or* commoner] explanation.
This is a pleasanter [*or* more pleasant] house, on a narrower [*or* more narrow]
    street.

If in doubt, use *more* rather than *-er*. Using *more* where *-er* is usual sounds less strange than using *-er* where *more* is usual.

The comparative form of adverbs is sometimes formed by adding *-er* (or just *-r* if the adverb ends in *-e*), but is usually formed by using *more* or *less:*

Later in the day it started to rain.
She writes more clearly than her sister.
He goes running less often in the winter.

To say that two things are equal in some specified way, use *as . . . as:*

The nylon shirt is as expensive as the cotton one.
He can't run as fast as his brother.

To say that two things are unequal, you can use *more . . . than* or *less . . . than* and also *not as . . . as* or *not so . . . as:*

These shoes are more comfortable than my old ones.
My new apartment is not as [*or* not so] big as my old one.

You can make the comparison stronger by adding a word such as *even, much, far,* or *nearly*:

> These cookies are even better than the cake.
> The second part of the test was much [*or* far] easier than the first part.
> The second part of the test was not nearly as hard as the first part.

With *as . . . as,* you can add words such as *just* or *equally* for emphasis:

> German cars are just [*or* equally] as reliable as Japanese ones.

For emphasis, *not as* can be replaced by *nowhere near as* or *nothing like as*, especially in informal speech:

> This soup is nowhere near as good as the one you made yesterday.

✓ Check

1. Comparisons using *this* and *that*

Write a sentence using each noun and adjective given. Change the adjective into its comparative form, and compare the noun to "that one."

Examples: car, clean   This *car* is *cleaner* than that one.
                         song, rhythmic This *song* is *more rhythmic* than that one.

1. class, quiet   _____

2. house, clean   _____

3. city, important   _____

4. book, long   _____

5. coat, beautiful   _____

6. movie, interesting   _____

7. child, happy   _____

8. carpet, thin   _____

9. building, modern   _____

10. painting, expressive   _____

2. Comparisons of Nouns

Write a sentence using each set of nouns and adjective. Compare the first noun to the second noun, using the adjective in its comparative form.

Example: Rome/beautiful/Milan
                → Rome is more beautiful than Milan.

1. Blue flowers/unusual/white   _____

2. Green peppers/tasty/red peppers   _____

3. Lions/dangerous/house cats   _____

4. Jane/young and fit/her husband   _____

5. Tuesdays/good/Fridays for me   _____

3. *as . . . as, more . . . than, less . . . than*

Fill in the blanks using *as . . . as, not as . . . as,* **or** *than.*

Example: This meeting is ____ ____ interesting ____ the last one.
                → This meeting is not as interesting as the last one

1. Easter is just ____ special ____ Christmas to me.

2. He thinks driving on the right is more difficult _____ driving on the left.

3. The bananas are selling for less money here _____ they are at that store.

4. Going by horse is ____ ____ quick _____ going by car.

5. The film is nowhere near ____ good _____ the book.

6. William is already ____ tall ____ his mother.

7. This class is far harder _____ the other class.

8. I am _____ trustworthy _____ she is.

9. This cake is not ____ good ____ the cake she made.

10. These exercises weren't nearly ____ hard _____ the previous ones.

12 It's the ~~modernest~~ building ~~of~~ the city.

most modern ... *in*

Forming superlatives is very similar to forming comparatives (Unit 11).

To form the superlative of a long adjective, use *the most* or *the least:*

> The roses are the most beautiful flowers in your garden.
> He thinks San Francisco is the most interesting city in California.

For most short adjectives, add *-est* and use *the* before it. If the adjective ends in *-e*, just add *-st.*

> Philip's sisters are tall, but Philip is the tallest child.
> This is the longest novel he has written.
> All your shirts are nice, but the blue one is the nicest.

For a one-syllable adjective ending in a consonant preceded by a single vowel, double the consonant before adding *-est*: *mad → maddest, slim → slimmest,* etc.:

> That boy has the saddest face I've ever seen.

The same two-syllable adjectives that take *more* or *less* also take *most* or *least*. The others take *-est.*

> All the houses on this street are fairly modern, but yours is the most modern.
> This is the most basic fridge that you can buy.
> Julia is the cleverest girl in the class.

For two-syllable adjectives ending in *-y*, change the *y* to *i* and add *-est:*

> This is the loveliest house in the whole village.
> He's the happiest baby I've ever known.

If in doubt about a two-syllable adjective, use *most* rather than *-est.*

A few common short adjectives have irregular superlatives:

bad → worst	many → most
far → farthest *or* furthest	much → most

12 : It's the ~~modernest~~ *most modern* building ~~of~~ *in* the city.

good → best   well → best
little → least

A superlative often isn't followed immediately by a noun, since the noun may have been stated before:

I've had many bad meals in the U.S., but that one was the worst.

It is also possible for a superlative to be followed by an *of*-phrase stating what things are being compared:

Mr. Fallows is the nicest person I've met here. → Mr. Fallows is the nicest of the people I've met here.
The most beautiful sister was Jane. → The most beautiful of the three sisters was Jane.

A noun that follows the superlative is often followed by *of* or *in*. When talking about a place (as in the title sentence above), we use *in*.

She was the smartest member of the family.
Everest is the highest mountain in the world.

To say that something is part of a superlative group, you use "one of" before "the most . . ." or "the least . . ." and a plural noun:

Tokyo is one of the most expensive cities in the world.

"By far" is often used for emphasis:

New York is by far the biggest city in the U.S.

Superlative adverbs are treated similarly:

We all slept late, but I slept the latest.
His argument was the least clearly stated of them all.
We're enjoying the most rapidly expanding economy in years.

1. Superlatives with -*est* or *most*

Write a sentence using the cues given, changing the adjective into its superlative form.

Example: The dog / big / animal in the house.
                → The dog is the biggest animal in the house.

1. The Chrysler Building is / unusual / building in New York.

    _____

2. The *Mona Lisa* is / famous / painting in the Louvre.

    _____

3. Lisa is / tall / girl in our class.

    _____

4. Pelé is / famous / soccer player of all time.

    _____

5. We live on / quiet / street in the town.

    _____

6. Albert Einstein was one of / influential / scientists ever.

    _____

7. It was / steep / mountain I had ever climbed.

    _____

8. This is / good / cake.

    _____

9. She is / lovely / woman I've ever seen.

    _____

10. This one is / good / of the lot.

    _____

13 Our house is <u>big enough</u> ~~enough big~~ and has <u>enough bedrooms</u> ~~bedrooms enough~~.

Enough is often an adjective. The adjective *enough* usually goes before a noun:

> Do we have enough bread?
> There aren't enough plumbers in Chicago.
> There's enough space for all the furniture.
> There isn't enough yellow paint.
> Do you have enough large nails for the job?

When *enough* is an adverb, it always follows a verb, adjective, or adverb:

> Those nails aren't large enough. [*not* enough large]
> She hasn't worked enough to earn a vacation. [*not* enough worked]
> Is Harry strong enough to lift it? [*not* enough strong]

Enough may also be a pronoun:

> There was enough for all of us.
> By now she had had enough of his lies.

Whether it is used as an adjective, adverb, or pronoun, it is often followed by a *to*-infinitive:

> There aren't enough buses to take all these people.
> I'm hungry enough to eat a horse.
> They have enough to survive the winter.

Too is often compared with the adverb *enough*, because it has an almost opposite meaning. *Too* always goes before the adjective that it modifies:

> Is Harry too weak to lift it?
> Those nails are too large.

Notice that *too* is often used with a *to*-infinitive, but with *too* (unlike *enough*) there must be an adjective before the *to*-infinitive.

Too much and *too many* are often used in contrast to *enough*:

I definitely drink enough water—maybe I drink too much.
There are enough teachers in the U.S.; some people think there are too many.

✓ Check

1. Complete the Sentences

Use *enough* and *too* to complete the sentences below.

1. Do we have _____ bread? Yes—in fact, we have too much.

2. There aren't _____ plumbers in Chicago.

3. Do you have _____ large nails to do the job?

4. There is _____ paint for all the students.

5. Those nails aren't large _____ to do the job.

6. Is Harry strong _____ to lift it?

7. I think my son is _____ fat.

8. Isn't it _____ cold to go swimming?

9. There are _____ many students in the class.

10. There aren't _____ students in the class.

2. Answer the Questions

Use the cues to answer the questions negatively. Use *too* or *enough* in the answer.

Examples: Can I drive down this street? - car / wide
               No, the car is too wide.
               Can he reach the switch? - he / tall
               No, he is not tall enough.

1. Can we go to Australia for a vacation? - plane fare / expensive

   _____

2. Can I plant flowers here? - soil / poor

   _____

3. Can we solve the problem? - we / clever

   _____

13 : Our house is ~~enough big~~ *big enough* and has ~~bedrooms enough~~ *enough bedrooms*.

4. Can we take the table home? - it / heavy

    _____

5. Can you buy this car? - I / rich

    _____

6. Can we go in the swimming pool? - water / cold

    _____

7. Can we play on the lawn? - grass / wet

    _____

8. Can you carry that suitcase for me? - I / strong

    _____

9. Will he apply for the job? - he / experienced

    _____

10. 10. Do you think she will go to the party? - she / busy

    _____

3. Make Conversations

Write conversations using the cues. Use *enough* in your question, and use both *enough* and *too* in your answer, as in the example below.

Example: teachers / the U.S.
          Are there enough teachers in the U.S.?
          Yes, there are enough teachers; in fact, there are too many.

1. water / reservoir _____

    _____

2. milk / cake batter _____

    _____

3. books / shelves _____

    _____

4. chairs / hall _____

    _____

5. people / lecture hall _____

_____

                    such a
14 He is a ~~so~~ good friend.

So and *such* are often confused by learners.

The adverb *so* generally modifies an adjective, which is usually followed by a *that*-clause that expresses the result of the first clause:

> The weather was so bad that we stayed at home.
> My truck is so wide that it can't go down that street.

So is often used with *much, many, little,* and *few*:

> The crowd was making so much noise that I couldn't hear the speaker.
> There were so many people in the bar that we couldn't get in.
> These shirts cost so little that I'm going to buy ten of them.
> So few people came that the concert was canceled.

So can also be used as simply an emphatic way of saying "very":

> That man is so annoying.
> The weather was so beautiful!

It can also modify another adverb:

> The man spoke so quietly that I couldn't hear what he said.

So is also often used as a conjunction, meaning "thus" or "therefore." You will rarely confuse the conjunction and the adverb.

> The day was lovely, so she decided to go for a swim.

Such is generally used to modify a noun or an adjective. These two uses can look almost identical. Before a singular count noun, *such* is always followed by *a* (or *an*).

> He's such an idiot!
> Those guys are such cowboys.
> That's such a stupid idea!
> They're such strong animals.

Such, meaning "so much," can be used immediately before a noncount noun:

> We had such fun at the beach.
> They had such trouble finding our house.

Such can be confused with *so* when it is used before a *that*-clause expressing a result. But *such* is only used before an adjective if a noun follows the adjective:

> The party made such a noise [*or* so much noise] that they called the police.
> The news was such a shock [*or* so shocking] that she fainted.
> They're such intelligent students that I never give any of them a bad grade.
> The party was so noisy [*not* such noisy] that they called the police.

✓ Check ───────────────────────────────

1. Change *So* to *Such*

Change the *so*-sentences to *such*-sentences, as in the example.

Example: The man was so foolish that he lost all his money.
                  → He was such a foolish man that he lost all his money.

1. The woman was so beautiful that everyone looked at her.

   _____

2. The car was so old that no one bought it.

   _____

3. The children are so naughty that they can't be left alone.

   _____

4. The book was so long that it took me a year to read it.

   _____

5. The package is so heavy that mailing it will be too expensive.

   _____

2. Change *Such* to *So*

Change the *such*-sentences to *so*-sentences, as in the example.

Example: He was such a clever boy that he easily passed all his exams.
→ The boy was so clever that he easily passed all his exams.

1. It was such bad weather that they canceled the parade.

   _____

2. He was such an unpleasant man that no one liked him.

   _____

3. She was such a quiet girl that everyone ignored her.

   _____

4. It was such a bad storm that all the crops were ruined.

   _____

5. Those are such rare drawings that they're insured for $100,000.

   _____

15 He knows he can't write ~~good~~ *well*.

The sentence above shows the error of putting an adjective where an adverb should go.

Adverbs usually modify verbs, but they may also modify adjectives, other adverbs, prepositions, and even complete clauses and sentences:

He often plays tennis on Saturdays.
She sang that song beautifully.

They went up the stairs as quietly as they could.
The plan was beautifully simple.
The weekend passed too quickly.
The ball rolled almost to the edge.
Today we have exams.

Most adverbs are formed by adding *-ly* to an adjective. When the adjective ends in *-y*, the *y* usually changes to *i* when *-ly* is added.

quick → quickly
nice → nicely
careful → carefully
guilty → guiltily

But many of the most common adverbs are not formed with *-ly*:

again	more	there
also	never	today
always	not	too
as	now	very
even	often	well
ever	sometimes	when
here	soon	where
how	then	why
just		

Some adverbs are spelled the same as their adjectives. Most of these do not end in *-ly*. The most useful ones include the following:

far	late	right
fast	loud	slow
hard	more	straight
early	quick	wrong

He's a fast driver. → He drives fast.
They were hard workers. → They worked hard.

For almost all adverbs, you form the comparative with *more*, and the superlative with *most* or *the most*:

> He behaves more confidently than his brother.
> It rains most often in the months of January and July.
> This novel is the most beautifully written of the three.

But for a few one-syllable adverbs, you form the comparative with *-er* and the superlative with *-est*:

> People can work harder in cooler climates.
> People work [the] hardest when they feel needed.
> He hits the ball higher than most golfers.
> In his school days he always jumped the highest and ran the fastest.

The adverb from *good* is *well*; the adverb from *bad* is *badly*. *Well* and *good* have the same comparative and superlative forms (i.e., *better* and *best*), and *badly* and *bad* have the same comparative and superlative forms (i.e., *worse* and *worst*).

> He's a good player, but he didn't play well last night.
> It wasn't a bad idea, but it was badly planned.
> Joanne plays the cello well. She plays better than Alice. She plays the best of
>   anyone in the orchestra.

Learners sometimes put an adjective where an adverb should go, or an adverb where an adjective should go. The most common mistake is to use *good* in place of *well*. Adverbs are also sometimes used improperly after verbs that describe the senses and feelings.

> They want to learn English quickly. [*Not*: They want to learn English quick.]
> She felt different from the other students. [*Not*: She felt differently from the other
>   students.]
> She felt the dog's neck gently. [*Not*: She felt the dog's neck gentle.]
> He looked closely at the small animal. [*Not*: He looked close at the small animal.]
> Be careful with that computer. [*Not*: Be carefully with that computer.]
> The music seems too loud. [*Not*: The music seems too loudly.]
> He looked handsome in his new suit. [*Not*: He looked handsomely in his new suit.]

Some adjectives end in *-ly*, including *friendly, lovely, likely, elderly, holy, silly, ugly*, and *deadly*. And a few *-ly* words, such as *daily, early, monthly, weekly*, and *yearly*, may be either adjectives or adverbs.

✓ Check

1. Fill in the Blanks

Fill in each blank with an adverb formed from the adjective in parentheses. Some sentences require the comparative or superlative form of the adverb.

Example: Her family greeted her ___warmly___ . (warm)

1. The plan was _____ simple. (beautiful)

2. She was _____ disappointed by his decision. (cruel)

3. He stated his opinion more _____ than his brother. (confident)

4. I think this novel is the most _____ written of the three. (imaginative)

5. They went up the stairs as _____ as they could. (quiet)

6. You can drive _____ once we are out of the city. (fast)

7. He hits the ball _____ than most golfers. (high)

8. During gym class, she always jumped the _____ and ran the _____.
    (high, fast)

9. She works very _____. (hard)

10. Joanne plays piano quite _____. (good)

11. She plays _____ than Alice. (good)

12. She is always the _____ prepared member of the orchestra. (good)

13. Mark drives _____. (bad)

14. He drives even _____ when he's tired. (bad)

15. That car is the _____ designed car that I have ever seen. (bad)

2. Adjective to Adverb

Rewrite the sentences using adverbs rather than adjectives, as in the example.

Example: He's a very slow driver
                   → He drives very slowly.

1. She's a beautiful singer. _____

 2. He's a quick learner. _____

 3. They are good dancers. _____

 4. She describes things in a very clear way. _____

 5. They are bad swimmers. _____

 6. We are hard workers. _____

 7. He's a faster runner than his brother. _____

 8. She's a slower speaker than her sister. _____

 9. He treated his dogs in a cruel way. _____

 10. His handling of the negotiations was smooth. _____

16 It's a two *two-door* ~~doors~~ car.

When an adjective contains two or more words, they are **usually connected by** hyphens.

Such adjectives are generally formed from phrases. If **the phrase has a plural noun, the** noun becomes singular when used in an adjective:

> The van has five doors. / It's a five-door van.
> The girl we met is six years old. / We met a six-year-old girl.
> His scar is three inches long. / He has a three-inch-long scar.

This is also true for nouns with irregular plurals:

> It's a job for two men. / It's a two-man job.
> The shark that killed her was ten feet long. / She was **killed by a ten-foot-long** shark.

For parts of the body, -*ed* is usually added to the noun (and its final **consonant is doubled** if it immediately follows a single vowel letter):

> Hydra was a monster with many heads. / Hydra was a **many-headed monster.**
> Spiders have eight legs. / Spiders are eight-legged creatures.

The man who chased me had one arm. / I was chased by a one-armed man.
He described her as having green eyes and red hair. / He described her as green-eyed and red-haired.

Hyphens are also used for many adjectives that don't include count nouns.

> a well-known professor
> the Anglo-Dutch oil company
> her light-green skirt
> this long-delayed event
> their middle-aged audience
> an 18th-century idea
> his well-to-do family

Some adjectives lose their hyphens when they follow the noun they modify:

> The professor was well known.
> The event had been long delayed.

The meaning of most hyphenated adjectives is obvious; those that cannot be easily understood can usually be found in a dictionary.

✓ Check ───────────────────────────

1. Phrases to Adjectives

Rewrite the sentences by turning phrases into adjectives, as in the example.

Example: There are four horses in the race.
                  → It's a four-horse race.

1. The bottle holds two liters.

   It's _____.

2. The boat is for three men.

   It's _____.

3. The tattoo on her back is ten inches long.

   She has _____.

4. The man who followed us had long hair.

We were followed by _____.

5. The woman I was introduced to had blue eyes and fair hair.

I was introduced to _____.

2. Adjectives to Phrases

Rewrite the sentences by turning the adjectives into phrases, as in the example.

Example: It's a four-horse race.
     → There are four horses in the race.

1. Octagons are eight-sided figures.

Octagons are figures that have _____.

2. Humans are two-legged creatures.

Humans are creatures that have _____.

3. We saw an eighty-year-old turtle.

The turtle _____.

4. He was wounded by a two-foot-long arrow.

The arrow that wounded him was _____.

5. We need a twenty-man team.

We need a team _____.

17 They lived in a ~~brick white old~~ house.

an old white brick

The order in which adjectives are placed in a sentence may vary, but some rules about ordering are always observed.

Most of the time, an adjective precedes the noun it describes.

  They had just taken a difficult History test.

However, most ordinary adjectives may also follow a noun subject and its verb:

> The History tests were always difficult.

Many nouns, in their singular forms, may be used like adjectives. When they function this way, they are called *attributive adjectives* or simply *attributives*. Attributives always precede the nouns they modify.

> his research paper
> a lemon drink
> the apartment building [*not* the apartments building]

Ordinary adjectives and attributive adjectives are often used together to modify a single noun. Any ordinary adjectives always precede any attributives. (The attributive adjectives in the following examples are shown in italics.)

> a moist, rich *chocolate* cake
> new *work safety* rules
> the experienced *summer baseball league* staff

Notice that attributives, unlike ordinary adjectives, are never separated by commas.

Adjectives before a noun are usually listed in a particular order. Any article (*a, an, the*), demonstrative adjective (*this, that,* etc.), indefinite adjective (*another, half,* etc.), or possessive adjective (*my, their,* etc.) comes first. If there is a number, it comes first or second.

> a small window
> that lively dance
> some easy questions
> her first success
> four middle-aged men

Following these, adjectives generally come in the following order:

> *opinion word* → *size* → *temperature* → *age* → *shape* → *color* → *nationality* → *material*

Opinion adjectives include such words as *attractive, clever, delicious, excited, interesting,* and *ugly*; size adjectives include *deep, long,* and *narrow*; temperature adjectives include *cool* and *sweltering*; age adjectives include *new* and *fifty-year-old*; and so on. Here are some further examples (the attributives are shown in italics):

the old Russian coins
those first few words
his three clean shirts
overweight middle-aged *club* members
some interesting *industry* surveys
several attractive, large, dark-green, wooden chairs
our two large, blue-and-white cardboard *milk* cartons
a small, heavy, antique, round-bellied, black, Norwegian iron *wood* stove

✔ Check

1. Rearrange

Put the adjectives, attributives, and nouns in the right order.

1. education, annual, ninth, conference, the _____

2. dresses, new, two, her _____

3. small, tables, some, yellow, wooden _____

4. Chinese, urns, enormous, two _____

5. flower, an, purple, jungle, exotic _____

2. Rewrite the Sentences

Rewrite these sentences, putting the adjectives in the proper order.

1. She introduced us to old three charming Thai restaurants.

   _____

2. It was an ancient large Chinese yellow ginkgo tree.

   _____

3. He was interested in a dirty old brass Arabian lamp.

   _____

4. They spent long three cool summers in the mountains.

   _____

5. The college built large a wooden dormitory new student.

   _____

3. Fill in the Blanks

Arrange these sets of adjectives in the preferred order for their sentences.

Example: We went for a ride in   <u>his huge, brand-new, red</u>   sports car.
       (brand-new his huge red)

1. He showed us _____ sleigh.
   (green his wooden large splendid)

2. She saw a _____ vase.
   (slender purple glass 45-year-old)

3. I finally found copies of _____ books.
   (those British two delightful)

4. _____ coins are rare and valuable.
   (old your dirty all gold Spanish)

5. They were seeking _____ can.
   (antique small a watering Japanese)

18 He <u>approached</u> ~~carefully~~ *carefully approached* the building.

An adverb modifying a verb may often appear at different places in a sentence. An adverb often appears between an auxiliary verb and a main verb, especially when it is describing *how* some action is being done.

> We were driving slowly along the icy mountain road.
> We were driving along the icy mountain road slowly.
> We were slowly driving along the icy mountain road.

But an adverb may not be placed between a verb and its direct object (as in the title sentence above).

> The audience was enjoying the concert immensely. [*Not:* The audience was enjoying immensely the concert.]

An adverb that modifies an entire sentence may also be moved to **different places in the** sentence:

> She probably will be singing the lead role.
> She will probably be singing the lead role.
> Probably she will be singing the lead role.

But when an adverb modifies an adjective or another adverb, it should be placed immediately before the other word:

> He seemed especially happy last night. [= Last night he seemed happier than he usually seems.]
> He seemed happy, especially last night. [= He seemed happy in general, and seemed even happier than usual last night.]

✓ Check

Reorder the Sentences

Move the adverb in each sentence to its best position. The phrases in parentheses can help you decide where to place the adverb.

Example: The sack landed with a thud heavily. (the sack landed very hard)
→ The sack landed heavily with a thud.

1. The travel agent planned perfectly our entire vacation. (the travel agent did a good job planning the vacation)

2. The story that they told us was moving extraordinarily.

3. We drove along slowly the icy mountain road.

4. He was a better seldom player than his cousin. (his cousin usually played better)

5. I felt tired especially this morning. (I felt more tired this morning than I usually do)

19 *Can you*
~~Do you~~ can meet me at the restaurant?

The meaning of modal auxiliaries can sometimes be difficult to understand. But the grammar of modals is also sometimes difficult, especially when a modal is used with another auxiliary.

The modal auxiliaries—*can, could, may, might, must, ought to, shall, should, will,* and *would*—are generally used to express something other than simple fact. They are often used in statements and questions about permission *(may, can, could)*, possibility *(may, might, could, would)*, necessity *(must, shall, will)*, intention *(will, must, would)*, advice *(should, ought to)*, ability *(can, could)*, and prediction *(will, shall, would)*.

> They told her that she could visit them next weekend.
> He might rather go to a nightclub.
> War between the two countries must be prevented.
> She said she would never marry again.
> You shouldn't say things like that to your father.
> Good tires can last for more than 80,000 miles.
> She will win the election easily.

Most modal auxiliaries have only one form, their basic infinitive form; they never end in *-ing, -ed,* or *-s.* A modal is almost always followed by a verb in its infinitive form. (Another word may come between the two words.) But neither infinitive ever includes *to;* that is, *to* never comes before or after the modal auxiliary, except in the special case of *ought to.*

Many questions begin with *do, have, be,* or a modal auxiliary. But *do, have,* and *be* are never used before a modal auxiliary in a question clause.

> Can you spell your name for me? [*Not:* Do you can spell your name for me?]
> Should we take a bus or a taxi? [*Not:* Do we should take a bus or a taxi?]

Although modal auxiliaries never take different forms to express the tenses, they often combine with *have* to form a perfect tense called the *modal perfect. Have* is followed by a past participle, not an infinitive:

> They must have finished by now. [= I'm sure that they are finished now.]
> You should have told me where you were going. [= You didn't tell me where you were going, although I wanted you to tell me.]

She could have passed the test if she had studied harder. [= She didn't pass the test because she didn't study hard enough.]

He may have gone to a movie. [= It's possible that he went to a movie.]

Since modal auxiliaries don't change their form, they can't form all the possible tenses, and other words must be used instead.

✓ Check

1. Fill in the Blanks

Complete each sentence, using the modal perfect and a form of the verb in parentheses.

1. You should _____ _____ your boss about it. (tell)

2. Did you think that you could _____ _____ better yesterday? (play)

3. The bus might _____ _____ already. (leave)

4. She must _____ _____ to the movie by herself. (go)

5. They ought to _____ _____ that it was dangerous. (know)

2. Find the Errors

In the following sentences, cross out each error and write the correct word above it.

1. Can you finished all that work yesterday?

2. I will must complete this paper before next week.

3. Their children should to do more work in the house.

4. We want to can see the movie soon.

5. Should I to go to my doctor?

20 She *has* ha̶v̶e̶ a brother who *lives* l̶i̶v̶e in Mexico.

In English, unlike many other languages, one single verb form is often used for an entire tense:

I/you/he/she/it/we/you/they	talked	(simple past)
I/you/he/she/it/we/you/they	had talked	(past perfect)
I/you/he/she/it/we/you/they	will talk	(simple future with *will*)
I/you/he/she/it/we/you/they	will have talked	(future perfect)
I/you/he/she/it/we/you/they	will be talking	(future continuous with *will be*)

But in four tenses—the simple present, the present perfect, the present perfect continuous, and the past continuous—the third-person singular (*he/she/it*) takes a different form. And because there are so few changes to verb endings in English, students often forget to make the one change that there is!

In the simple present, *I/we/you/they* take the verb's basic infinitive form, but *he/she/it* take a form ending in *-s*.

they sing / he sings

Verbs ending in *-ch*, *-s*, *-sh*, *-x*, or *-z* add *-es*:

you fetch / it fetches
I miss / he misses
we wash / she washes
they box / he boxes
we waltz / she waltzes

Verbs ending in consonant + *y* change the *y* to *i* and add *-es* (but verbs ending in vowel + *y* just add *-s*):

I try / she tries
you annoy / he annoys

In two other cases—the present continuous and the simple future with *going to*—the third-person singular is not the only person that changes. In the past continuous, the first-person singular and the third-person singular are the same.

I am resting	you/we/they are resting	he/she/it is resting
I am going to call	you/we/they are going to call	he/she/it is going to call
I was laughing	you/we/they were laughing	he/she/it was laughing

✓ Check

1. Fill in the Blanks

Fill in the blanks by putting the verbs in parentheses into the simple present.

6. That bird _____ very well. (fly)

7. He _____ English fluently. (speak)

8. They _____ hard and _____ hard. (work, play)

9. How does she _____ to work? (go)

10. She doesn't _____ her mother very much. (help)

11. He _____ and _____ too much. (eat, drink)

12. Where do John and Louise _____? (live)

13. We _____ to help you. (want)

14. In this country it _____ all summer and _____ all winter. (rain, snow)

15. Mrs. Davis _____ all our meals and _____ the house. (cook, clean)

2. Find the Errors

Cross out each error and write the correct word above it.

1. She praies in church every morning before she gos to work.

2. That blender buzzs loudly but it mixs well.

3. When she applys the paint to the wall, this paper catchs the drips.

4. If you has the keys, please gives them to me.

5. He are going to travel in Italy while his wife staies home.

21 You are ~~drive~~ too fast.
driving

English, unlike most languages, has two tenses that deal with the present: the simple present and the present continuous. The sentence "You are drive too fast" uses a form that is neither one tense nor the other.

The present continuous is used for an action that is happening now. It is formed with *am/are/is* and the *-ing* participle:

> I am trying to help you.
> They are waiting to see the doctor.
> I'm not asking you—I'm telling you.
> She isn't sleeping well.
> Why am I doing this?
> Is it working?

The simple present is used to refer to the period of time that exists now, and to talk about general truths and actions that happen or are done regularly. It uses the infinitive form of the verb except in the third person singular, which normally adds *-s* to the infinitive:

> Dogs frighten me.
> Water boils at 212 degrees Fahrenheit.
> She works ten hours a day.
> They go to church every Sunday.
> He visits his parents most weekends.
> It is almost three o'clock.

Because it is used to talk about actions that occur regularly, the simple present is often used with adverbs such as *usually, seldom, rarely, often, always, never, ever,* and *sometimes* (called *adverbs of frequency*). These normally go right before the main verb:

> It never snows here.
> I rarely watch television these days.
> Her husband always cooks dinner on Sundays.
> She often works late.

Although the present usually isn't used for an *action* that is happening right now, several kinds of verbs are normally used in the present to describe a *state*, or situation, that exists at the present moment. They include:

- verbs expressing emotions: appreciate, care, desire, fear, hate, like, love, mind, prefer, value, want, wish, etc.

- verbs of mental activity: agree, believe, consider, expect, forget, guess, imagine, intend, know, notice, observe, perceive, realize, recall, recognize, remember, think, trust, understand, etc.

- verbs of possession: belong, have, own, possess, etc.

- verbs of the senses: feel, hear, see, smell, sound, taste, etc.

- miscellaneous other verbs: appear, be, concern, consist, cost, depend on, deserve, hold, include, involve, matter, mean, need, regard, remain, resemble, result, seem, suppose, etc.

> Do you like this dish? [*Not:* Are you liking this dish?]
> I think that's a good painting. [*Not:* I am thinking that's a good painting.]
> That book belongs to Harry. [*Not:* That book is belonging to Harry.]
> This sounds like a Nirvana song. [*Not:* This is sounding like a Nirvana song.]
> He agrees with us about the war. [*Not:* He is agreeing with us about the war.]

Note that the most common use of the present continuous is for talking informally about events in the near future:

> We are going to the game tonight.
> Are you coming with us?

For tables of these two tenses, see pp. 143–149.

✓ Check

1. Fill in the Blanks

Fill in each blank with the verb in parentheses in the simple present.

1. Daniel doesn't like white wine, but he sometimes _____ red wine. (drink)

2. He _____ on Drury Lane. (live)

3. Loud noises _____ the children. (scare)

4. Emma _____ in a restaurant. (work)

5. It _____ almost 3 o'clock. (be)

2. Complete the Conversation

Fill in the blanks in the following phone conversation, using only the present continuous forms of the verbs *read, do, watch,* **and** *write.*

Ann: What _____ you doing now?

Tom: I _____ _____ TV.

Ann: Is your wife _____ TV?

Tom: No, she _____ not.

Ann: Is she _____ a book?

Tom: No, she _____ not _____ a book; she _____ _____ a letter.

3. Make Sentences in the Simple Present

Make three conversations by using the cues below. Ask whether the person does the activity, then answer that they sometimes do one but never do the other.

Example: Jason and Joan / watch / movies, TV
                  Do Jason and Joan watch movies?
                  - They sometimes watch TV, but they never watch movies.

1. Jane / eat / meat, fish

    _____

    _____

2. Robert and Jim / drink / wine, beer

    _____

    _____

3. you / listen to / pop music, jazz

    _____

    _____

4. Make Sentences in the Present Continuous

Make three conversations by using the cues below. Ask whether the person is doing the first activity, then answer that he or she is instead doing the second activity.

Example: Mr. Lawson / fish, clean the garage
                Is Mr. Lawson fishing?
                - No, he's cleaning the garage.

1. David / work, read a book

_____

_____

2. Lucy and Clare / watch TV, listen to music

_____

_____

3. you / cut the grass, plant vegetables

_____

_____

22 I haven't ~~saw~~ ^{seen} him because he ~~haven't~~ ^{hasn't} come home yet.

The present perfect tense is formed with *have/has* and the past participle. For most verbs, the past participle ends in *-ed* and is identical to the verb's simple past form. But for some verbs (such as *speak*), the two forms are different.

> He studied all night and has studied most of the morning.
> She chose her gifts early, but I haven't chosen mine yet.

For a list of the common irregular verbs, see pp. 150–152.

The present perfect is used:

- To talk about past activities or states but in a time frame that is not over:

  > I have seen three films this month.
  > He has already smoked 20 cigarettes today.

> I've hated winter since I was a child.
> She's been here for half an hour.

These activities or states can still be modified (for example, by seeing another film before the end of the month or by smoking more cigarettes today). For past events within a time frame that has ended, we would use the simple past tense:

> I saw two films last month.
> He smoked 40 cigarettes yesterday.

- To talk about a past activity or state for which the time frame is vague, not specified, or unimportant:

> I've stayed at the Beverly Hilton Hotel three times.
> She has met his father but hasn't met his brother.
> Have you ever eaten caviar?

Again, these activities or states can still be modified (by staying at the hotel again, meeting the brother, or eating caviar for the first time). By contrast, the simple past tense talks about events at a definite time in the past:

> I stayed at the Beverly Hilton when I first came to the U.S.
> She met his father in 2006, but not his brother.
> I had my first caviar last night, but I didn't like it.

- To talk about an event that happened very recently and therefore affects the present. In this use, a sentence will often include *just*, *yet*, or *already*:

> He has just called the airline.
> I haven't finished my coffee yet.
> They've already done it.

- To talk about an event that happened at an unspecified time in the past.

> She has decided to accept the job offer.
> I have given them all the information I can.

The negative is formed by adding *not* (-*n't*) after *have*:

> We have not [*or* haven't] worked for a long time.
> She hasn't [*or* has not] told us what she needs.

Questions are formed by putting *have* before the subject:

> They have already voted. → Have they already voted?
> It has rained here this week. → Has it rained here this week?

For more on the present perfect, see Unit 23.

✓ Check ─────────────────────────────────

1. Fill in the Blanks

Complete each sentence using the verb in parentheses in the present perfect.

1. They _____ already _____. (arrive)

2. _____ it _____ here this week? (snowed)

3. We _____ not _____ too long, I hope. (stay)

4. She _____n't _____ us what she wants. (tell)

5. I _____ _____ three movies tonight. (watch)

6. He _____ just _____ the gas company. (call)

7. He _____ already _____ a cup of coffee. (have)

8. _____ you ever _____ this before? (do)

9. I _____ always _____ to go to Las Vegas. (want)

10. She _____ _____ the Prime Minister. (meet)

11. I _____ already _____ dinner. (finish)

12. They _____ already _____ they will go. (say)

13. She _____ _____ here for a half an hour. (be)

14. I _____ _____ this book before. (read)

15. She _____ _____ to finish her soup, but she's full. (try)

2. Answer the Questions

Answer each question below truthfully using the present perfect, in *one* of the ways given in the example.

Example: Have you ever eaten rabbit?
- Yes, I have eaten rabbit a few times/many times. *or*
- No, I have never eaten rabbit.

1. Have you ever drunk Chinese beer?

    _____

2. Have you ever flown across the equator?

    _____

3. Have you ever been to Australia?

    _____

4. Have you ever seen the Empire State Building?

    _____

5. Have you ever been really hungry?

    _____

3. *Has been* **or** *has gone?*

Fill in the blanks with *have gone, has gone, have been,* or *has been.*

1. _____ you _____ to lunch yet?

2. Is Mr. Smith in his office? No, he _____ _____ to the bank.

3. He _____ never _____ to our home.

4. _____ David _____ home yet or is he still here?

5. _____ Sarah ever _____ abroad?

23 I haven't ~~gone~~ to Mali but I h~~ave visited~~ Chad in 2006.

been *visited*

This unit looks at one of the hardest parts of English grammar: the difference between the present perfect (see Unit 22) and the simple past.

To review the difference between the two tenses, look at this conversation:

> *Ann*: Have you ever seen a whale?
> *Bob*: No, I've never seen a whale but I've seen dolphins.
> *Ann*: When did you see them?
> *Bob*: I saw them last year in California.
> *Ann*: What did you think of them?
> *Bob*: I thought they were wonderful.

The first two sentences are in the present perfect: "I've never seen a whale" may change, because Bob might see a whale next week. But in the last four sentences, the time is very specific; they are talking of an event that occurred in the past and cannot be changed. Thus, they use the simple past.

Here is another conversation:

> *Cathy*: How many times have you been to New York?
> *Dave*: Oh, I've been there lots of times.
> *Cathy*: When did you last go?
> *Dave*: I went six months ago.
> *Cathy*: What did you do there?
> *Dave*: I attended a medical conference.

The two tenses are used here in exactly the same way. The first two lines use the present perfect (since Dave may go to New York many more times in his life), and the last four lines use the past tense (since they are about facts that will not change).

Here is a third conversation:

> *Ella*: Have you seen the new Spielberg movie yet?
> *Fred*: No, I haven't seen it yet, but I saw Scorsese's new film.
> *Ella*: Where did you see that?

23 : I haven't ~~gone~~ ^{been} to Mali but I <u>have ~~visited~~</u> ^{visited} Chad in 2006.

Fred: I saw it at the new theater next to the bus station.
Ella: Did you enjoy it?
Fred: No, I hated it.

Again, the first part of the conversation is in the present perfect (since Fred may see the Spielberg movie in the future), but the rest is in the past tense (since the facts they are discussing will not change).

✔ Check ——————————————————

1. Fill in the Blanks

Finish each conversation by filling in the blanks with the correct forms of the verbs in parentheses.

Ann: _____ you ever _____ caviar? (try)

Bob: No, I _____ never _____ caviar, but I _____ sushi once. (try)

Ann: When _____ you _____ sushi? (try)

Bob: I _____ it last year. (try)

Ann: What _____ you _____ of it? (think)

Bob: I _____ it was great. (think)

Cathy: How many times _____ you _____ your parents this year? (visit)

Dave: I _____ _____ them lots of times. (visit)

Cathy: When _____ you last _____ them? (visit)

Dave: I _____ them two months ago. (visit)

Cathy: How _____ they? (be)

Dave: They _____ well, thanks. (be)

Ella: _____ you _____ his new novel? (read)

Fred: No, I _____n't _____ it yet, but I _____ his last one. (read)

Ella: When _____ you _____ it? (read)

Fred: I _____ it a few years ago. (read)

Ella: _____ you _____ his last book? (like)

Fred: No, I _____ it. (hate)

2. Make Conversations

Write a conversation using each subject given, as in the example. Use the words in bold in each answer.

Example: go to Chicago

> *Ann*: **Have you ever** been to Chicago?
> *Bob*: **Yes, I have** been to Chicago.
> *Ann*: **How many times have you** been there?
> *Bob*: **I have** been there **three times**.
> *Ann*: **When did you last** go to Chicago?
> *Bob*: **I last** went to Chicago in 2005.
> *Ann*: **Did you like** it?
> *Bob*: **Yes, I liked** it **very much**.

1. eat lobster

_____

_____

_____

_____

_____

_____

2. see the Rolling Stones

_____

_____

_____

_____

_____

_____

69

have been   *for*
24 : I ~~am~~ sitting here ~~since~~ two hours.

24 *have been* *for*
I ~~am~~ sitting here ~~since~~ two hours.

Learners of English often use the wrong verb tense with *for* and *since*.

The present perfect continuous ("have been sitting") is often used with both *for* and *since*:

>I've been working for two hours.
>I've been working since 3:30.

For is used with a period of time; *since* is used with a point in time.

>for two hours [=a period of time lasting two hours]
>for a while [=a period of time lasting a while]
>for a long time [=a period of time lasting a long time]
>since two o'clock [=a point in time starting at two o'clock]
>since 2004 [=a point in time starting in 2004]
>since the new year [=a point in time starting January 1]

For can often be omitted:

>I have been sitting here [for] half an hour.
>They've been working there [for] three years.
>It's been raining [for] two days.

Omitting *for* is usually perfectly correct, but sometimes it will make the meaning unclear, so it's often safer not to omit it.

For and *since* are also used with other tenses, especially the past perfect ("had sat") and the past perfect continuous ("had been sitting"). And *for* (but not *since*) is often used with the simple future tense ("will sit" or "be going to sit").

>We had waited since last Monday. / We had waited for hours.
>We had been waiting since last Monday. / We had been waiting for hours.
>We will wait here for another week if we have to.

Another time word that is sometimes used with the wrong tense is *ago*. *Ago* is used with the simple past tense, but never with the present perfect or present perfect continuous:

I'm sure he was in the office ten minutes ago. [*Not:* I'm sure he has been in the office ten minutes ago.]

✓ Check

1. Fill in the Blanks

Use the verbs in parentheses in the present perfect continuous.

1. We _____ _____ _____ here for twelve years. (live)

2. I _____ _____ _____ for forty-five minutes. (practice)

3. He _____ _____ _____ that book since last Christmas. (read)

4. They _____ _____ _____ golf since 8:00. (play)

5. We _____ _____ _____ for ten hours. (drive)

6. She _____ _____ _____ in this factory since 2001. (work)

7. They _____ _____ _____ the matter for the last three hours. (discuss)

8. It _____ _____ _____ since last Sunday. (snow)

9. You _____ _____ _____ that excuse for twenty years. (make)

10. He _____ _____ _____ that job since he was a teenager. (do)

2. *For, Since,* or *Ago?*

Fill in each blank with *for, since,* **or** *ago.*

1. It has been raining _____ seven hours.

2. We have been studying English _____ two years.

3. They have been working _____ lunch.

4. He just spoke to her ten minutes _____.

5. I have been collecting coins _____ 1992.

6. You've been writing that letter _____ three hours.

7. She met him six years _____.

8. I have been reading this chapter _____ nine o'clock.

have been *for*
24 : I ~~am~~ sitting here ~~since~~ two hours.

9. We have been waiting _____ ten days.

10. I have been living here _____ I was a child.

3. Make Sentences

Make one sentence out of each pair of sentences, as in the example.

Example: I arrived here two hours ago. I am still waiting here.
          → I have been waiting here two hours.

1. We started studying English ten years ago. We are still studying English now.

    _____

2. He got a job in New Orleans in 2004. He is still working there.

    _____

3. She sat down on that bench three hours ago. She is still sitting there.

    _____

4. I moved to this house when I was a child. I am still living here.

    _____

5. He began cooking 30 minutes ago. He is still cooking.

    _____

6. They started discussing that problem two days ago. They are still discussing it.

    _____

7. She started writing her thesis in 1998. She hasn't finished it yet.

    _____

8. You started following me twenty minutes ago. You are still following me.

    _____

9. They started building that bridge five years ago. They haven't finished it yet.

    _____

10. She started playing the piano when she was four. She still plays the piano.

    _____

25 By then, the guest of honor ~~left~~ *had left*.

Learners sometimes use the simple past tense when they should instead use the past perfect.

The past perfect, which is formed by using *had* and the past participle, is like "the past of the past." It is normally used either (1) for an action already completed by the time of another past action, or (2) for an action completed at some specific past time.

> Mary accepted a ride after she had walked several blocks in the rain.
> By 9:30, Mary had walked at least two miles.

It is also used (3) in conditional sentences, where it appears in an *if*-clause or with phrases such as *if only, as if,* or *as though*:

> If I had known that, I wouldn't have sent the letter.
> If I had done my homework exercises, I would have passed the test.
> If only she had had the time, she would have traveled to Senegal.
> He spoke about Rome as if he had lived there himself.

Note that the actions in the past perfect need not be in the distant past; they only must have occurred before a specified past time or event:

> She had had a very busy day and was happy finally to go to bed.
> We had hiked for hours by then.

Using the past perfect requires paying attention to the order of events in a sentence. This order is often indicated by such words as *after, at, before, by, early, in, on, last, later, next, once, then, until,* and *when.*

> They had gone to bed shortly before the storm began.
> The party had continued until dawn.

In negative sentences, *not* (or *-n't*) follows *had*:

> I hadn't talked to Joe before I went back to the farm.

25 : By then, the guest of honor *~~left~~*. [*had left* handwritten above]

In questions, *had* comes first:

> Had she told you about it before she left?

✓ Check

1. Make Sentences in the Past Perfect

Complete these sentences, using the verbs in parentheses in the past perfect tense.

1. I _____ _____ to the health club as soon as I finished work. (go)

2. Everybody _____ _____ for the day, so there was nobody at work. (leave)

3. Dave _____ _____ in Chicago as a boy, but he moved to New York when he was 18. (live)

4. Barbara immediately phoned her parents, who _____ _____ her missing. (report)

5. Years after it _____ _____ _____, the factory burned to the ground. (shut down)

2. Choose the Right Verb

In each sentence, underline the correct form of the verb.

1. a. Susan remembered everything as if it (happened / had happened) yesterday.

   b. Susan remembers everything that (happened / had happened) yesterday.

2. a. Why (hasn't / hadn't) the government solved the problem before it got so serious?

   b. Why (hasn't / hadn't) the government solved the problem by now?

3. a. They (lived / had lived) in Oregon for decades before moving to Iowa.

   b. They (lived / had lived) in Oregon for health reasons.

4. a. He (had taken / took) the dog for a walk in the park earlier that morning.

   b. He (had taken / took) the dog for a walk in the park today.

5. a. I asked if he (talked / had talked) to his doctor about it when he last saw him.

   b. I asked if he (talked / had talked) to his doctor regularly.

26 The church has offered ~~offer~~ meals to homeless people.

The special verbs called *auxiliary verbs* are *be*, *have*, *do*, and the modal verbs: *can*, *could*, *may*, *might*, *must*, *ought to*, *shall*, *should*, *will*, and *would*. (The modals are discussed in Unit 19.) An auxiliary verb is commonly used before another verb. The other verb always appears in its basic infinitive form except when it follows *have* or *be*.

Be, *have*, and *do* are mainly used as auxiliaries to express a verb's tense or the passive voice, to make a sentence negative, or to ask a yes/no question:

> She has been gone for a week.
> A message was handed to him by the waiter.
> This new strategy didn't work any better than the old one.
> Do they have any reason to believe it?

The auxiliary *do* is always used with a verb in the infinitive without *to*. *Do* may be used to express a negative meaning or to ask a question:

> Do they know the answer? – They don't know the answer.
> Did she know the answer? – No, she didn't know the answer either.

Do is also sometimes used to emphasize the main verb:

> He really does know the answer.

or to substitute for a verb that has just been used:

> We know the answer, and so does he.

Have is used with the past participle (not the infinitive) to form the perfect tenses (see Units 22 and 25):

> We've planted potatoes for at least ten years.
> She finally hung the picture that she had finished in February.

Be is used with the present participle (not the infinitive) to form the continuous tenses:

> He is building a house on a hill above the city.
> She was planning a long vacation abroad.

They'll be reading all of Jane Austen's novels next.

The modal verbs are always followed by an infinitive without *to*:

> If she keeps having lunch with Carl, her boyfriend might become jealous.
> That couldn't be true.
> No one can go into that room.
> Everybody must be at the meeting on Friday.
> All right, I'll do it myself.
> You shouldn't eat that unless it's fresh.

However, the main verb can usually be omitted if it has just been stated with its modal auxiliary:

> He will go, but she won't [go].

✓ Check

1. Choose the Right Verb

Underline the correct form of the verb.

1. A message (is / was) given to me.

2. Did they (planned / plan) to stay for the weekend?

3. He had (forget / forgotten) to lock the garage door.

4. He is (building / build) a house on a hill above the city.

5. She (be / may be) planning a long vacation abroad.

6. We (hope / hoping) that you will all come visit us soon.

7. I have (grown / grow) these kinds of vegetables for two years.

8. They had (arose / arise / arisen) an hour before breakfast.

9. The cat had (tore / torn) the newspaper soon after it came.

10. They have (took / taken) two trips to the mountains.

2. Action Matches

Underline the correct form of the verb.

1. Have you (wash / washed / washing) your face yet?

2. We could (go / going / gone) to the mountains later in August.

3. They (had / have) finished their assignment last week.

4. She could (spoke / speaking / speak) Chinese when she was young.

5. My cousin will (sends / send / sending) us postcards during his trip.

27 It was the most ~~depressed~~ *depressing* movie I've ever seen.

Participles are used to form the perfect and continuous verb tenses (see Units 21–25), but they may also be used as adjectives.

> Their boat was sinking quickly.
> Messages had been received from a sinking ship.
> The border has been closed.
> Sounds were coming from behind the closed door.

The present participle always ends in *-ing* (as in *eating*). The past participle usually ends in *-ed* (*stopped*), but may also end in *-d* (*told*), *-t* (*slept*), -or *-n* or *-en* (*known, fallen*), or it may be formed by a vowel change (*sung*). For regular verbs, the past participle is identical to the past tense; for irregular verbs, it is often different from the past tense (*began/begun, shook/shaken, wrote/written*, etc.). See the list of irregular verbs on p. 150.

As an adjective, a present participle normally describes the person or thing causing some result, while a past participle describes the effect of some action:

> It was a depressing book.
> Mike was a depressed young man.
> The plot was confusing.
> Andrea's mother is often confused.

Both participles may precede the noun, and both may follow a linking verb (*be, become, seem*, etc.):

> We could hear the breaking waves.
> One of the front windows was broken.
> The local children liked to skate on the frozen lake.

77

27 : It was the most ~~depressed~~ *depressing* movie I've ever seen.

The wind was freezing.

There are phrases and sentences in which both participles could make sense and be grammatically correct. However, changing the type of participle always changes a sentence's meaning:

> The children avoided the neighbors' frightening dog. / He tried to comfort the frightened dog.
> She had growing children to care for. / Her grown children had moved away.
> They watched the falling leaves in the afternoon sun. / Fallen leaves covered the path.
> There's something annoying about my roommate. / My roommate is annoyed at me.
> He's sick of school and says his teachers are boring. / There's nothing to do, and we're all bored.
> They had read alarming reports about the abuse of refugees. / They were alarmed by reports of the abuse of refugees.

Since *-ed* endings may be hard to hear, be careful not to make the mistake of omitting them (as in "She is very experience").

✓ Check

1. Present vs. Past

For each exercise, write a sentence for the present participle and another for the past participle, using the situation in parentheses.

Example: amusing / amused (they are watching short films that they think are funny)
→ They watched several *amusing* short films.
→ They were *amused* by several short films.

1. fascinating / fascinated (they are looking at an interesting painting)

_____

_____

2. frightening / frightened (she is talking about a scary movie)

_____

_____

3. irritating / irritated (he is talking about his brother, whom he doesn't like)

_____

_____

4. moving / moved (I am listening to a speech and am enjoying it)

_____

_____

5. satisfying / satisfied (we had a very good meal)

_____

_____

2. Choose the Right Participle

Underline the correct participle.

1. His talent was so (amazed / amazing) that people came from far away to hear him play.

2. Did you watch that (interesting / interested) history show on TV last night?

3. I was (surprised / surprising) to see how popular American music is around the world.

4. He filled the (washing/washed) machine with his clothes.

5. The (astonishing / astonished) reporter was left speechless by the actor's remarks.

28 I ~~was living~~ in France, but I left in 2002.

used to live

To say that something occurred regularly, or over a period of time, in the past and is now finished, you can use the auxiliary *used to* and a verb infinitive.

> They used to be quite rich, but now they're almost poor.
> She's an atheist now, but she used to believe in God.

used to live (handwritten above "was living")

These days he wears jeans and a T-shirt to work, though he used to wear a suit.

Used to contrasts the past with the present. The simple past may be used instead, especially with *once, formerly,* or *previously*:

> They were once quite rich, but now they're very poor.
> She's an atheist now, but she formerly believed in God.
> He wears jeans and a T-shirt to work, but previously he wore a suit.

Don't confuse the auxiliary *used to* with the phrasal verbs *be used to* and *get used to*, which mean "be accustomed to" and "become accustomed to" (see Unit 50):

> She's used to hearing that she looks like Meryl Streep.

The negative form of *used to* is *didn't use to*. *Didn't use to* is common in informal conversation but not in writing.

> I'm surprised he ate those mushrooms—he didn't use to like them.

The past continuous describes an action that started before a particular point in the past and continued after that point:

> At two o'clock I was waiting at the airport.
> At this time last Sunday we were lying on a beach.
> He was living in Venice at the start of the war.

The past point in time can often be a past action; this action is expressed with the simple past. Thus, the past continuous often describes a background state or action, during which a past event or action occurred.

> They were living in Amsterdam when the war started.
> It was still raining when they left the theater.

While can often be used if *when* is omitted:

> The war started while they were living in Amsterdam.
> They left the theater while it was still raining.

Notice that replacing the past continuous tense in the main clause with the simple past changes the meaning of the sentence:

> *past continuous* + when + *simple past*:
> We were having dinner when he arrived. [= While we were having dinner, he arrived.]

> *simple past* + when + *simple past*:
> We had dinner when she arrived. [= We had dinner just after she arrived. = She arrived, and then we had dinner.]

✔ Check

1. Can You Remember?

Fill in the blanks, using the verbs in parentheses and "used to" (where it is appropriate).

1. They _____ in town but now they _____ in the country. (live)

2. She _____ to church when she _____ younger. (go, be)

3. He _____ a blue car, but now he _____ everywhere instead. (drive, walk)

4. When I _____ a child I _____ my bike every Saturday. (be, ride)

5. After dinner we _____ for the concert to begin. (wait)

6. Last Sunday we _____ lying on a beach. (be)

7. He _____ living in Europe a few years ago. (be)

8. I _____ whenever my mother _____ squash for lunch. (complain, cook)

9. While I was _____, my cell phone _____. (drive, ring)

10. My boss _____ at me every day, but she _____ last year. (yell, stop)

81

28 : I was ~~living~~ _used to live_ in France, but I left in 2002.

2. Fill in the Blanks

Complete each sentence, using the verb in parentheses in the past continuous or with *used to*.

Examples: He _____ in Venice at the start of the war. (live)
→ He was living in Venice at the start of the war.
When I was a child I _____ to church every Sunday. (go)
→ When I was a child I used to go to church every Sunday.

1. I _____ Republican but now I'm a Democrat. (vote)

2. He _____ me his life story when the doorbell rang. (tell)

3. I _____ him when we were in school together. (like)

4. While I _____ , I reread her letter. (wait)

5. My mother _____ to us every night when we were children. (read)

3. Rewrite the Sentences

Rewrite the sentences, using *used to* or the past continuous.

Examples: We were having dinner when he arrived.
→ While we were having dinner, he arrived.
When I was young I lived in France.
→ I used to live in France when I was young.

1. I'm a doctor now; I was a nurse before that.

   I used _____

2. When it started to snow, we were playing tennis.

   While _____

3. While the guards were sleeping, the prisoner escaped.

   When the prisoner _____

4. When we were in Florida, we went to the beach every day.

   We used _____

5. I hated studying before I went to college.

   Before _____

29 I will tell him when I ~~will~~ *See* him tomorrow.

In the sentence above, clauses about two future events are separated by *when*. The *when-*clause talks about the future, but the clause's correct verb is in the present tense.

The sentences below are similar. The clause that follows a "time word" (such as *when, before, after,* and *as soon as*) talks about the future, but its verb is in the present:

> She will see your brother next week when she goes [*not* will go] to Texas.
> He will talk to them before he makes [*not* will make] a decision.
> It probably won't happen until after they elect [*not* will elect] a new president.
> As soon as I have [*not* will have] some information, I'll call you.

The same thing happens in these *if*-clauses:

> If I see [*not* will see] your sister, I will tell her to come home.
> We will send you a postcard if we go [*not* will go] to London.

See Units 31 and 32 for more on conditional sentences such as these.

The perfect tenses work in the same way. In time clauses that begin with *when, before, after, as soon as,* or *by the time,* the present perfect is used, not the future perfect:

> I will have finished the ironing before you have finished [*not* will have finished] the washing.
> I will send you the report after I have read [*not* will have read] it.
> The meal will have been eaten by the time you have sat [*not* will have sat] down.

The simple present is used as often as the present perfect in such situations:

> I will have finished the ironing before you finish the washing.
> I will send you the report after I read it.
> The meal will have been eaten by the time you sit down.

29 : I will tell him when I ~~will~~ _see_ him tomorrow.

✓ Check

1. Can You Remember?

Fill in the blanks using the verbs in parentheses in the correct tense.

1. She _____ them next week when she _____ home. (see, go)

2. He _____ to them before he _____ town. (talk, leave)

3. I _____ you as soon as I _____ any more news. (call, have)

4. If I _____ your sister, I _____ her to call you. (see, tell)

5. She _____ us the money when she _____ her paycheck. (give, get)

6. I _____ the cleaning if you _____ the kids. (finish, watch)

7. Our boss _____ us a new assignment after we _____ this one. (give, finish)

8. The law probably _____n't _____ until after Congress _____ its session. (pass, resume)

9. By the time you _____ this, I _____. (read, leave)

10. If you _____ me the truth, I _____ not _____ angry. (tell, get)

2. Fix the Errors

Cross out each verb that is in the wrong tense and write the correct tense above it.

1. I will talk to you before you will have your interview.

2. We will write to you as soon as we will hear from the manufacturers.

3. As soon as John will arrive, he will call you.

4. I will take a photo of the snow before it will disappear.

5. When I will see Rose next week, I will give her your message.

3. Fill in the Blanks

Fill in the blanks using the verbs in parentheses in the correct tense.

1. If you _____ your grandfather, you _____ him very happy. (visit, make)

2. We _____ a big meal before you _____. (have, leave)

3. Everything _____ ready when the guests _____. (be, arrive)

4. I _____ her a call before I _____. (give, forget)

5. We _____ as soon as you _____ ready. (leave, be)

6. We _____ a picnic if it _____. (not have, rain)

7. I _____ you when I _____ the answer. (tell, know)

8. We _____ straight to the beach as soon as we _____. (go, arrive)

9. I _____ the car if it _____ cheap enough. (buy, be)

10. I _____ glad when the exams _____ over. (be, be)

30 We recommend that you ~~are~~ *be* prepared.

The subjunctive is used in several ways, including in conditional *if*-clauses (Units 31 and 32) and for expressing wishes (see Unit 33). This unit discusses the use of the subjunctive for requests and suggestions.

Requests and suggestions use the present subjunctive. The present subjunctive is very simple, since it uses only the basic infinitive form of the verb (*feel*, *drive*, etc.). That is, the verb does not change to show the subject's person or number (including the third-person singular).

The present subjunctive is generally used in clauses that begin with *that*, usually after one of the following verbs:

ask
decide
demand
insist
intend
order
propose
recommend
request

require
suggest
urge

It is used even when the request or suggestion occurred in the past.

She asked that he drive [*not* drives] more slowly.
He insisted that the work be [*not* is] finished on time.
We recommend that you be [*not* are] prepared for the interview.
The government has requested that he send [*not* sends] more documents.
They are suggesting that she teach [*not* teaches] algebra.

Negative requests or suggestions are expressed by using *not* before the verb:

We recommend that you not be late for the interview.
They are suggesting that she not teach algebra this semester.

These kinds of requests and suggestions can also be formed with *should* and the infinitive.

He insisted that the work should be finished on time.
The government has requested that he should send more documents.
They are suggesting that she should teach algebra.

The subjunctive is also used in a few common expressions that never change. In the following sentences, several of these are shown in italics. (All these phrases can be found in a dictionary.)

It would be his last work—his swan song, *as it were.* [= if I may express it in that way]
Far be it from me [= it would be inappropriate for me] to tell you how to raise your children.
It will probably be expensive, but *be that as it may* [=regardless of that], we'll all support it.
So be it [=I accept the situation]—I won't object any further.
Come what may [=regardless of what happens], we're determined to complete the entire journey.
Suffice it to say [=all that I need to and am willing to say is] that the show was a disaster.
God bless you! [= I hope that God will bless you.]
Heaven forbid! [= I hope that heaven (God) prevents that.]
Heaven help us! [= I hope that heaven (God) will help us.]

✓ Check

1. Choose the Right Tense

Underline the verb in the correct tense.

1. The principal is suggesting that the new teacher (teaches/teach) geometry.

2. The rules require that everyone (leave/leaves) their weapons outside the building.

3. She recommends that you (are/be) prepared for anything.

4. He asked that she (drives/drive) slower through this neighborhood.

5. She insisted that the entire project (be/is) completed on schedule.

2. Fill in the Blank

Complete the common subjunctive expressions using a form of the verb in parentheses.

1. He's the head honcho, as it _____. (be)

2. Far _____ it from me to tell you how to run your business. (be)

3. Suffice _____ that the wedding was fantastic. (say)

4. I know you don't want to go. _____ that as it may, however, you have no choice. (be)

5. _____ what may, I won't miss the funeral. (come)

31 If I ~~would live~~ *lived* here, I would run every day.

Conditional sentences talk about a cause and a result (or effect). However, they do not state the cause and result as ordinary facts. Instead, both the cause and the result may be probable events, possible events, unlikely events, or impossible events.

The cause is expressed in a clause that begins with *if.* The result is expressed in a clause that almost always includes a modal auxiliary:

87

31 : If I ~~would~~ *lived* live here, I would run every day.

If he hurries, he can still catch the bus.
If you're right, then I'm wrong.
If we get rich, we'll eat nothing but chocolate.
If I lived by the sea, I might learn to sail.
She would go back to college if she didn't have any children.
If I won the lottery, I could buy you a house.
He would understand the problem if he were a woman.

As you can see, conditional sentences can talk about the past, present, or future. Conditional sentences can also talk about events that are likely and events that are only possible. All these differences—between likely and merely possible events, and between past, present, and future events—require different forms of the sentence's verbs.

If something is certain or likely to happen if something else happens, we usually use the present tense in the *if*-clause and the future tense (with *will*) in the result or effect clause. This is sometimes called the Conditional I.

If you give me the keys, I'll start the car.
If he asks her, she'll say yes.
If the temperature reaches 400 degrees, the whole thing will explode.

If the result or effect is only a possibility, the *if*-clause uses the past tense, and the result clause uses *would* and the infinitive form of the verb. This is sometimes called the Conditional II.

If he asked her, she would say yes.
If you wanted it, I would buy it for you.

To be completely accurate, the tense in the *if*-clause is actually the past subjunctive rather than the past tense. But the past subjunctive is identical to the past tense except in one verb (the verb *be*), and today many native speakers ignore this difference completely.

If we are talking about something that didn't occur even though it was a possibility, we use the past perfect tense in the *if*-clause, and *would have* in the result clause. This is sometimes called the Conditional III.

If they had come, they would have had fun.
He would have been hurt if he hadn't moved quickly.

In the next unit we will discuss the conditional further.

 Check ──────────────────────────────────

1. Fill in the Blanks

Fill in the blanks using the verbs in parentheses in the correct tense.

1. If I _____ by the sea, I _____ to swim. (live, learn)

2. If I _____ the lottery, I _____ my job. (win, quit)

3. If I _____ daughters, I _____ them after my aunts. (have, name)

4. If he _____ about it, he _____ the joke. (think, understand)

5. If I _____ you, I _____ to college. (be, go)

6. I _____ not _____ him if I _____ you. (believe, be)

7. If we _____ near the mountains, we _____ every day. (live, hike)

8. If she _____ more time, she _____ it for you. (have, do)

2. Make Sentences

Change the sentences below from declarative statements to conditional statements.

Example: I don't live near the sea. I haven't learn to swim.
                    → If I lived near the sea, I would learn to swim.

1. I am not going to Paris, so I won't visit your sister.

   _____

2. I'm not young, so I'm not going to run the Boston Marathon.

   _____

3. I'm not you, so I'm not going to wear that red dress.

   _____

4. I don't have a car, so I won't drive to Mexico.

   _____

5. I don't need a new radio, so I'm not going to buy a Sony.

    _____

6. I am not as pretty as my sister, so I am not very happy.

    _____

7. I don't have a beach house, so I don't go to the ocean every week.

    _____

8. He hasn't asked her to marry him, so she hasn't said yes.

    _____

9. She doesn't earn much money, so they are not going on vacation.

    _____

10. You don't like fish, so we don't go to that restaurant.

    _____

3. Write Positive and Negative Sentences

Make two conditional sentences, one positive and one negative, from each set of cues below.

Example: go / France / climb / Mont Blanc
                → If I went to France, I would climb Mont Blanc.
                → Even if I went to France, I wouldn't climb Mont Blanc.

1. be / thinner / wear / that dress

    _____

    _____

2. have / $20,000 / buy / new car

    _____

    _____

3. live / in Manhattan / go / to the theater every week

    _____

    _____

4. speak / German / live / Austria

_____

_____

5. need / new computer / choose / laptop

_____

_____

32 If she ~~would have~~ *had* seen it, she would have told me.

The result (or effect) clause of a conditional sentence sometimes uses a modal auxiliary other than *will* or *would*. In Conditional I, all the modals can be used. In Conditionals II and III, *could* and *might* can be used as well.

> If a storm hits, it might be dangerous.
> If it's 10:00, we must have slept about twelve hours.
> If you came to Seoul with me, we could visit Japan as well.
> If we weren't so busy all the time, we could read more.
> If I had known you wanted a camera, I could have bought you one in Hong Kong.
> If Johnson had played, we might have won.

Using *might* rather than *would* or *could* usually indicates that a possibility is less likely.

Negative conditional sentences are common:

> If I had realized that you already had one, I wouldn't have bought another.
> She would never have learned the truth if she hadn't read that letter.
> If they hadn't known him, they would never have helped him.
> You wouldn't have saved all that money if you hadn't bought the car from me.
> If they can't go tonight, they can go tomorrow instead.

Though *if* is by far the most common word for introducing conditional clauses, several other terms are used as well:

32 : If she ~~would~~ *had* ~~have~~ seen it, she would have told me.

Unless we solve the problem now, it's going to last for years.
As long as he doesn't fail this final test, the university will probably let him stay.

In Unit 31 we stated that the Conditional II actually uses the past subjunctive rather than the past tense, but that the only difference involves the verb *be*. *Be* in the past subjunctive always takes the form *were*, even after *I* and in the third person singular:

If I were working there, I would find another job.
If he were a little less lazy, his house would look a lot nicer.
If the side door were larger, we could move the piano through it.

But many native English-speakers use *was* instead of *were* in such cases:

If I was working there, I would find another job.
If she was a little less lazy, her house would look a lot nicer.
If the side door was larger, we could move the piano through it.

✓ Check

1. Fill in the Blanks

Fill in the blanks using the verbs in parentheses in the correct tense.

1. If I _____ that, I _____ with you. (know, go)

2. If she _____ not _____ that job, she _____ bankrupt. (get, go)

3. If you _____ the car last month, you _____ a lot of money. (buy, save)

4. If the team _____ won, we would _____ to the finals. (have, go)

5. If the van _____ larger, we _____ more people with us. (be, take)

2. Make Sentences

Change the sentences below from declarative statements to conditional statements.

Example: I didn't read books when I was a child, so I didn't learn to spell.
→ If I had read books when I was a child, I would have learned to spell.

1. I didn't work hard at school, so I didn't pass my exams.

_____

2. He didn't live near the ocean, so he didn't learn to swim when he was a boy.

    _____

3. I didn't train, so I didn't run the marathon.

    _____

4. My parents didn't have a car, so I didn't learn to drive.

    _____

5. She didn't find him, so she was unhappy.

    _____

6. The shirts weren't made of cotton, so I didn't buy one.

    _____

7. Mary didn't try, so she didn't beat John.

    _____

8. Lucy got up late, so she missed her flight.

    _____

9. I lost my temper, so I lost my job.

    _____

10. He fumbled the ball, so the other team scored a goal.

    _____

3. Make Positive and Negative Sentences

Write two past conditional sentences, one positive and one negative, using each set of cues below.

Example: buy a paper yesterday / know the result of the election
    →If I had bought a paper yesterday, I would have known the result of the election.
    → If I hadn't bought a paper yesterday, I wouldn't have known the result of the election.

1. read the report / understand the situation

    _____

    _____

2. have the money / buy a suit

    _____

    _____

3. need a secretary / hire you

    _____

    _____

4. know you were making dinner / come home

    _____

    _____

5. think about the problem / make the right decision

    _____

    _____

33 She wishes you ~~live~~ *lived* nearer.

The verb *wish* is generally used to express a desire for something. Thus, it very often expresses regret.

If you are unhappy about a current situation or state, you use the simple past tense for the verb after *wish*:

>   I wish this shop opened on Sundays.
>   I wish my job was in Newport.

After *wish*, *were* can be used instead of *was*. This is one of the few examples of the subjunctive in English.

>   I wish my job were in Newport.
>   She probably wishes she were ten years younger.

See Unit 31 for examples of the subjunctive after *if*.

Wish is commonly used with *would*:

> I wish he wouldn't make so much noise in the morning.
> I wish she wouldn't smoke while she's driving.
> She wishes you would help her more often.
> I wish he would leave.

To express regret about something that happened in the past, the past perfect is used for the verb after *wish*:

> I wish I had worked harder when I was in school.
> He wishes he hadn't gotten married so young.

Wish is used before a noun for rather formal expressions of good feeling:

> We wish you a happy retirement.
> I wish you happiness in all that you do in the future.

Wish and *hope* are often confused by learners. However, *hope* is almost never used to express regret. When expressing a desire for the future, the verb that follows *hope* may be in either the simple present or the simple future:

> I hope she visits her parents soon.
> I hope she'll visit her parents soon.

When talking about the present, it must be in the present continuous:

> I hope she's visiting her parents now.

When talking about the past, it may be in the simple past tense:

> I hope she visited her parents.

✔ Check ───────────────────

1. Fill in the Blanks

Fill in the blanks using the verbs in parentheses in the correct tense.

1. I wish we _____ happier. (be)

2. I wish my office _____ closer to my house. (be)

3. I wish you _____ something—your silence is killing me. (say)

4. She wishes she _____ a novelist. (become)

5. I wish I _____ harder in school. (try)

2. Express Regrets About the Present

Rewrite each sentence to express regret.

Example: I don't live near my parents.
          → I wish I lived near my parents.

1. I don't earn a lot of money.

_____

2. I am not as tall as my sister.

_____

3. I don't own a good tennis racket.

_____

4. I don't have a car.

_____

5. I'm not you.

_____

6. I can't swim.

_____

7. I don't have a house in the country.

_____

8. I can't afford a new coat.

_____

9. I'm not 20 years old.

_____

10. I am not going with you.

_____

3. Express Regrets About the Past

Rewrite each sentence to express regret.

Example: I didn't work hard when I was in school.
                → I wish I had worked hard when I was in school.

1. I didn't win the cup.

    _____

2. I didn't catch the last train.

    _____

3. I didn't run the marathon.

    _____

4. I didn't read books when I was a child.

    _____

5. I didn't learn to swim when I was a boy.

    _____

6. I didn't buy any presents.

    _____

7. I lost his address.

    _____

8. I got up late this morning.

    _____

9. I lost my temper.

    _____

10. I crashed my dad's car.

    _____

34 English is spoken
One ~~speaks~~ English here.

Many languages have a phrase like "One speaks English here." But in English itself, we use the passive voice instead of the impersonal "one."

The passive is formed with a form of *be* and the past participle:

> English is spoken here.
> The castle was built in the 16th century.
> These pieces were written by Clara Schumann.

It is often used to emphasize the action itself rather than the one doing it. Often the "doer" is not even mentioned:

> All our cars are designed in Italy and manufactured in China.
> The grapes are always picked in September.
> The painting was stolen in 1942 and found twenty years later.

When you turn an active sentence into a passive sentence, the sentence's direct object normally becomes its subject. If the doer is mentioned, it appears in a *by*-phrase:

> A gangster killed him. → He was killed by a gangster.
> A wasp had stung her. → She had been stung by a wasp.

Unlike in some other languages, the person or thing that the action was done to or for can also become the subject:

> A letter was given to Harry. → Harry was given a letter.
> A check was sent to the office. → The office was sent a check.
> A job in the sales department was offered to me. → I was offered a job in the sales department.

They, *you*, and *someone* can be used to avoid using the passive. In such cases, *they* and *you* don't refer to any particular person or people but instead mean simply "people." *One* is sometimes used instead of *you*, but more often in Britain than in the U.S.

> A black glove was handed in. → Someone handed in a black glove.
> Portuguese is spoken in Brazil. → They speak Portuguese in Brazil.

A shredder is used to destroy documents. → You use [=One uses] a shredder to destroy documents.

Many passive sentences include a modal verb:

He could be killed if he isn't careful.
These rugs must be cleaned.

Notice that there is a passive infinitive:

The Grand Canyon must be seen to be believed. [= A person must see the Grand Canyon in order to believe it.]
The winner is likely to be announced today. [= It is likely that the winner will be announced today.]

A common mistake is to say "I am born" in a sentence like "I am born in Vienna." In English you always say "was born" or "were born":

I was born in Vienna, but my children were born in the U.S.

✓ Check

1. Complete the Sentences

Change each sentence from active to passive.

Example: They brew this beer in Germany.
            → This beer is brewed in Germany.

1. They recounted the votes three times.

   The _____

2. Millions of people have seen this film.

   This _____

3. They will sell tons of cards this Christmas.

   Tons _____

4. They sell a thousand houses every year.

   A thousand _____

5. They had sold the painting by the time I arrived.

   The _____

6. They are building a new bridge across the river.

   A _____

7. Someone sent me this letter ten days ago.

   I _____

8. You use this knife to chop vegetables.

   This _____

9. Someone gave her a diamond ring for her birthday.

   She _____

10. Moths made these little holes.

    These _____

2. Active to Passive

Change the sentences into the passive.

1. Once you have opened the jar, you should refrigerate it.

   _____

2. By the time I got up, somebody had washed the dishes.

   _____

3. They're going to knock down these houses and widen the road.

   _____

4. Someone will change your sheets and clean your room once a week.

   _____

5. Someone had hit him over the head and stolen his wallet.

   _____

35 When ~~begins the class~~?
does the class begin

Learners often have trouble with several features of questions. One of them is the use of auxiliaries.

Questions in English exist in two types: *yes/no questions* and *wh- questions*. Yes/no questions can be answered with "yes" or "no"; *wh-* questions require many different kinds of answers.

Yes/no questions always begin with an auxiliary verb (*do, have, be,* or one of the modal auxiliaries), or with a form of *be* that is not functioning as an auxiliary verb. *Have* and *be* are used for the perfect and continuous tenses, as in ordinary statements. But for the simple present, simple past, or simple future, *do* is required. *Do* is always followed by the infinitive form of the verb.

> Have you ever lived in the city? (Yes, I lived there when I was 18.)
> Are you cold? (No, I'm fine.)
> Was it hard to tell your mother? (No, she was very understanding.)
> May we use this room for a meeting? (No, another meeting is about to begin.)
> Would you like to see a play instead? (Yes, that would be better than a movie.)
> Did anyone hear the scream? (Yes, the man upstairs did.)

In a *wh-* question, the first word begins with *wh-* or *h-*: *why, where, when, what, which, who, whom, whose,* or *how.*

> What time is it?
> Who told you about the decision?
> Whom was she calling?
> Whose computer have you been using?
> Which road do you usually take?
> How can we help you?
> Why would someone do that?
> When will the election be held?
> Where did you put the keys?

Wh- questions usually require an auxiliary verb (*be, have, do,* or a modal verb) before the main verb. There are two exceptions: (1) when *be* acts as the main verb rather than as an auxiliary, and (2) when the *wh-* word is the subject of the sentence:

> Which book is yours?
> Which costs more?

When *how* begins a question, it is usually followed by an adjective: *how many, how long, how often,* etc.:

How old are you?	I'm twenty-five [years old].
How wide is this road?	It's twenty feet wide.
How fast can those little cars go?	They can go 80 miles an hour.
How much land do you own?	We own five acres.

Notice that, in "How old are you?" both the question and the reply use *be*, rather than *have* (as in some other languages).

✓ Check

1. Complete the Sentences

Complete the sentences, using the verbs in parentheses in the correct tense.

1. When do we need _____? (leave)

2. How many bananas did you _____ today? (eat)

3. Have you ever _____ Greece? (visit)

4. Would you like _____ some more ice cream? (have)

5. _____ it difficult to turn down the job? (be, *past tense*)

6. When do you think we _____ there? (go, *future tense*)

7. Who _____ you the secret? (tell)

8. Where _____ you _____ the keys? (put, *past tense*)

9. How _____ you feeling? (be)

10. Can we _____ some ice cream? (have)

2. Choose the Right Verb

Underline the correct verb.

Example: <u>Can</u>/Do/Are we go to the store?

1. Have/Are/Do you tried her pie yet?

2. Did/Had/Was you hear what I said?

3. How old are/have/do you?

4. To whom are/have/do you speaking?

5. What have/are/do you done?

36 He ~~told~~ *said* that he ~~is~~ *was* hungry.

The title sentence shows how the tense must change in a **reported statement.**

To express what someone said, you may use *direct speech*, giving the person's **exact words** in quotation marks:

> "I'm staying at the Phoenix Hotel," Richard said.
> She said to her mother, "I bought a new car yesterday."
> Wendy said to me, "I'll be here again tomorrow at the same time."

Or you may use *reported*, or *indirect, speech*, giving the meaning of what was **said but not** the exact words. *That* is often used before the reported speech, but it may **usually be omit-**ted.

> Richard said [that] he was staying at the Phoenix Hotel.
> She told her mother [that)]she had bought a new car the day before.
> Wendy told me [that] she would be there again the next day at the same time.

As you see, the tense of the verb in indirect speech is usually "one tense back" from direct speech. Thus, "am staying" becomes "was staying," "bought" becomes "had bought," and "will be" becomes "would be."

However, if the reporting verb (*tell, say, ask,* etc.) is in the present tense or the **present per-**fect, the tense of the indirect speech doesn't change:

> Richard says [that] he is staying at the Phoenix Hotel.
> Richard has said [that] he is staying at the Phoenix Hotel.
> Wendy tells me [that] she will be there again tomorrow at the same time.
> Wendy has told me [that] she will be there again tomorrow at the same time.

Notice how other words in the indirect speech often need to change. These include not only personal pronouns and possessive adjectives (*I, me, my, mine, you, your, yours, we, us, our,* and *ours*) but also references to time: "today" may become "that day," "tomorrow" may become "the next day," and "yesterday" may become "the day before." Words that change may also include references that involve place: "this," "these," and "here" may need to change when they are reported.

> "This book just doesn't answer my questions," he complained.
> He complained that the book just didn't answer his questions.
> "We thought you would be coming today," she said.
> She said that they had thought we would be coming that day.

Say and *tell* are common in sentences with reported speech. The two words are very similar, but *tell* requires an indirect object:

> He told her that he was Canadian. [*Not:* He told that he was Canadian.]
> "I'm Canadian," he told her. [*Not:* "I'm Canadian," he told.]
> He told her that he was Canadian, and she told her parents.

Say does not take an indirect object. However, the person listening often becomes the object of a *to*-phrase.

> He said that he was Canadian.
> He said, "I'm Canadian."
> He said to her that he was Canadian.

For more on reported speech, see Units 37 and 38.

✔ Check

1. *Said* **or** *Told?*

Fill in each blank with *said* **or** *told.*

1. He _____ to her that he was sorry.

2. He _____ that he was sorry.

3. He _____ her he was sorry.

4. "I'm going to the concert," Peter _____.

   5. Judy _____ her mother that she had bought a new dress the day before.

   6. Wendy _____ to me, "I'll be going to the store again tomorrow."

   7. Wendy _____ me that she would be going to the store the next day as well.

   8. Peter _____ that he was going to the concert.

2. Direct Speech to Reported Speech

Change the direct speech to reported speech, as in the example.

Example:　　　Michael said to Anne, "I saw James yesterday."
　　　　　　　→ Michael told Anne that he had seen James the day before.

   1. Tim said to Jenny, "I'm in London."

   _____

   2. Sarah said to Alice, "I will be in New York tomorrow."

   _____

   3. Max said to Harry, "I have a pain in my leg."

   _____

   4. Her brother said to Elizabeth, "David works for Sony."

   _____

   5. My mother said to me, "Your sister is ill."

   _____

   6. Jane said to Tom, "It was raining earlier."

   _____

   7. Mr. and Mrs. Wilson said, "We have been waiting for two hours."

   _____

   8. The twins said to their teacher, "We don't want to be in the same class."

   _____

   9. My father said to me, "My company is losing money."

   _____

10. Peter said to Laura, "The weather was awful yesterday."

_____

3. Reported Speech to Direct Speech

Change the reported speech to direct speech, as in the example.

Example: Michael told Anne that he had seen James the day before.
             → Michael said to Anne, "I saw James yesterday."

1. My mother told me that she had been worried for several months.

_____

2. Her brother told Elizabeth that he had gotten married two weeks before.

_____

3. Tim told Jenny that he was in love with her.

_____

4. Mr. and Mrs. Wilson told me that I could stay with them.

_____

5. Peter told Laura that he had lost his job.

_____

6. My brother told me that he would be back the following week.

_____

7. Sarah told Alan that his wife had a problem.

_____

8. Jane told Tom that there was a man there to see him.

_____

9. Max told Harry that the police wanted to speak to them.

_____

10. The twins told their teacher that they were ill.

_____

37 He asked where ~~is my~~ *my mother was* ~~mother.~~

Reporting questions often leads to errors. Look at these two direct questions:

> Jane asked, "Where have you put my coat?"
> "Is the house near the sea?" David asked.

Now see how they are expressed as reported, or indirect, questions. Notice three things: the change of word order, the change of tense, and the use of *if* in the second sentence:

> Jane asked where I had put her coat.
> David asked if the house was near the sea.

These two examples show the two basic kinds of question in English. One kind begins with a question word: *what, when, where, which, who, why,* or *how.* When reporting a question that begins with a question word, the question clause begins with the same question word:

> What will you say to your mother? → He asked me what I would say to my mother.
> When is she seeing them again? → He asked when she would be seeing them again.
> How did you meet her? → He asked me how I had met her.

The other kind begins with an auxiliary verb (*do, be, have, will, must, could, can, would, may, might, shall, should,* etc.), and expects "Yes" or "No" for an answer. To report a yes/no question, you use *if* or *whether:*

> Are you feeling okay? → He asked if I was feeling okay.
> Did she live in Paris for a long time? → I asked her whether she had lived in Paris for a long time.
> Can they stay with you tonight? → She asked if they could stay with me that night.

In ordinary questions, the word order is: (*question word +*) *auxiliary + subject + verb.* (Notice that an auxiliary comes before the subject.)

> Where do you live?
> Why did the sales manager leave early?

Are you staying at the Royal Hotel?
Should they really go out in such bad weather?

But in reported questions, the word order for the question itself is: *question word* / if or whether + *subject* + (*auxiliary* +) *verb*. (Notice that an auxiliary verb follows the subject.)

He asked me where I lived.
She asked me why the sales manager had left early.
I asked if they were staying at the Royal Hotel.
She asked if they should really go out in such bad weather.

As in reported statements, the original verb tense in reported questions usually changes: *live* becomes *lived, did leave* becomes *had left*, and so on.

For more on reported speech, see Units 36 and 38.

✔ Check

1. Change the Direct Questions to Reported Questions

Rewrite the sentences as in the example.

Example: "How are you feeling, Tom?" Jane asked.
                    → Jane asked Tom how he was feeling.

1. "Where is Alice?" Jenny asked.

_____

2. "Have you ever read *Hamlet?*" Peter asked.

_____

3. "What will you do, Max?" Helen asked.

_____

4. "Which company does David work for?" his brother asked.

_____

5. "Will you be home soon?" my mother asked me.

_____

6. "Who lives here?" John asked George.

   _____

7. "How long have you been waiting?" they asked.

   _____

8. "Will we be in the same class?" the twins asked the teacher.

   _____

9. "Why did you tell her a lie?" my father asked.

   _____

10. "Is it a good hotel?" Paul asked Laura.

   _____

2. Change the Reported Questions to Direct Questions

Rewrite the sentences as in the example.

Example: Jane asked Tom how he was feeling.
                 → "How are you feeling, Tom?" Jane asked.

1. James asked Daniel where his house was.

   _____

2. Carl asked me if I had ever heard a Beethoven sonata.

   _____

3. Emma asked Mark what he would say to his mother.

   _____

4. His sister asked Bob which dessert he would like.

   _____

5. My father asked me if I would be late.

   _____

6. Barry asked Mrs. Gray which days she worked.

   _____

7. Mr. Johnson asked if I was thirsty.

    _____

8. The brothers asked their mother if she would wait for them.

    _____

9. My sister asked me why I wouldn't help her.

    _____

10. Matthew asked Rachel if the party the night before had been good.

    _____

38 He told me don't do it.

Reporting commands and instructions is usually simple. In the title sentence, however, the two basic ways of reporting, *direct* and *indirect*, have been combined.

Ordinary commands and instructions always use the verb's basic infinitive form:

> Go home!
> Sit here next to me.
> Combine the milk and eggs, and add the flour.

For negative commands and instructions, you simply add "Do not" or "Don't":

> Don't do it!
> Do not forget to lock the door.
> Don't laugh when I tell you this.

A command can easily be turned into a request: by adding a tag question such as "will you?" "would you?" or "could you?" (see Unit 44) or by starting the sentence with "Would you" or "Could you" or "Please."

> Please close the door.
> Answer the phone, will you?
> Could you close the door?
> Would you answer the phone, please?

Reporting a direct command is exactly like reporting a direct statement or question.

> "Have a seat," she said.

To report an indirect command or instruction, we usually use *tell* (or occasionally an emphatic word such as *command* or *order*). It is followed by the indirect object and a *to-infinitive*.

> Sit down! → She told her dog to sit down.
> Please come in. → He told me to come in.

To report a negative command, instruction, or request, we add *not* before the *to*-infinitive:

> Don't say a word. → She told him not to say a word.
> Don't be afraid. → He told me not to be afraid.

Reported requests usually use *ask* (or sometimes an emphatic word such as *beg*). Reported negative requests include *not* before the *to*-infinitive.

> Would you answer the phone, please? → He asked her to answer the phone.
> Would you buy some eggs? → She asked me to buy some eggs.
> Please don't hurt him! → She begged them not to hurt him.

✔ Check

1. Rewrite

Change these sentences from direct commands to reported commands or from reported commands to direct commands, using the words in parentheses, if any.

Examples: Don't sit there! (she, me)
                → She told me not to sit there.
                He told me to get out.
                → Get out!

1. She told me not to say a word. _____

2. He told the dog not to do it. _____

3. Sit down! (she, him) _____

4. Go home! (they, us) _____

5. Don't come in, please. (he, me) _____

6. Don't say a word. (she, him) _____

7. Don't do that! (they, us) _____

8. She asked us to close the door. (please) _____

9. He politely asked me to answer the phone. (please, would) _____

_____

10. Close that door. (she, him) _____

11. Answer the phone, please. (he, me) _____

12. He requested that I not see her again. (please) _____

_____

13. Could you fill out these forms for me? (she, me) _____

_____

14. She begged me not to hurt him. _____

15. She told me to buy her a ticket _____

2. Change the Direct Speech to Reported Speech

Change the direct commands to reported commands.

Examples: "Sit down, Tom," Jane said.
    → Jane told Tom to sit down.
    "Would you open the door please, Jack?" Sarah said.
    → Sarah asked Jack to open the door.

1. "Go away, Alice," Robert said.

_____

2. "Children, stand up!" the teacher said.

_____

3. "Don't open the window, Paul!" Maria said.

_____

4. "Ann, please come back home," her mother said.

_____

5. "Would you speak to your mother please, Peter?" his aunt asked.

_____

6. "David, don't let her do it," John said.

_____

7. "Ian, would you please give me a call?" said his sister.

_____

8. "Don't spend all your money!" my uncle said.

_____

9. "Carol, would you please help?" Judy said.

_____

10. "Don't let anybody into the house, girls," their father said.

_____

3. Change the Reported Speech to Direct Speech

Change the reported commands to direct commands.

Examples: Jane told Tom to sit down.
            → "Sit down, Tom," Jane said.
            Sarah asked Jack to open the door.
            → "Would you open the door, please, Jack," Sarah asked.

1. Maria told Paul not to disturb her.

_____

2. Their uncle told the children not to leave the house.

_____

3. Robert asked me to answer the phone while he was out.

_____

4. John told David not to invest in the scheme.

_____

5. Their father told the girls not to stay out late.

_____

6. His mother politely asked Peter to buy her some milk on his way home.

_____

7. Her aunt begged Jane not to leave.

_____

8. Judy asked Carol to be her bridesmaid.

_____

9. The teacher told the children to be quiet.

_____

10. His sister asked Ian nicely to give her a lift to work.

_____

39 *want to* I ~~want~~ speak English but I can't ~~to~~ ~~speak~~ English.
speak

Many verbs may be followed by a *to*-infinitive. However, only a few verbs may be followed by an infinitive without *to*; the most common of these are the auxiliary *do* and the modal auxiliaries (*can, could, may, might, must, ought to, shall, should, will, would*).

The main verb usually follows the auxiliary immediately, but an adverb (including *not*) may come between them:

> It could take several days.
> Next year they might be living somewhere else.
> You should slowly remove the cover.
> The thieves didn't wait for the police.

In questions, the subject comes between *do* and the main verb:

> Does this mean that the fighting is over?
> Didn't you go to Brazil last year?

A very few other verbs may be followed by an infinitive without *to*. The most common are *feel, hear, help, let, make, see, watch,* and *have* (as a regular verb rather than as an auxiliary). Each of these verbs always takes a direct object before the second verb:

> She felt it crawl up her leg.
> They're watching the ships come into the harbor.
> I'll have her e-mail you when she arrives.
> His parents made him call the neighbors and apologize.
> Don't let the kids leave without taking their lunches.
> The doorman will help you get a taxi.

✔ Check

Fill in the Blanks

Complete the sentences, using the verbs in parentheses as *to*-infinitives and infinitives without *to*.

1. I hear she might _____ home tomorrow. (come)

2. She wants _____ what you thought of the play. (know)

3. He saw the bug _____ up the wall and jumped up _____ it. (crawl, kill)

4. Do you think we should _____, or should we _____ on without him? (wait, go)

5. Do you _____ Italian? (speak)

6. I would like _____ Italian. (learn)

7. You can't make me _____ broccoli. (like)

8. Is she in? Will you _____ her _____ me when she does get in? (have, call)

9. I need _____ a quick shower before we leave. (take)

10. They made him _____ home before midnight. (promise, come)

40 She finished her paper and handed ~~in it~~. *it in*

Phrasal verbs are two-word (or sometimes three-word) verbs that consist of an ordinary verb with an adverb or a preposition (or both an adverb and a preposition). Most phrasal verbs have a meaning that is very different from the meaning of the ordinary verb by itself.

The first word of a phrasal verb changes form like a normal verb, while the second word (and the third word, if there is one) never changes:

> We're hanging on for now.
> We were still trying to hang on.
> We hung on for as long as possible.

Some phrasal verbs are transitive and require a direct object; others are intransitive and never take an object; still others have both intransitive and intransitive meanings.

An intransitive phrasal verb never takes another word between its two (or three) parts:

> The cake she was baking turned out well. [*Not*: The cake she was baking turned well out.]
> They ended up on a plane to Uganda. [*Not*: They ended on a plane to Uganda up.]
> Things like this go on in many companies. [*Not*: Things like this go in many companies on.]

Transitive phrasal verbs do not all behave the same way. Some of them, like intransitive phrasal verbs, cannot be separated:

> The peasants had taken up arms against the king. [*Not*: The peasants had taken arms up against the king.]
> That morning he came across the document [*Not*: That morning he came the document across.]

However, most transitive phrasal verbs may be separated. If the object is only one word long, it usually goes inside the phrasal verb; if it is two words long, it may or may not go inside it; if it is longer, it usually follows the verb.

> It can be difficult to tell twins apart.
> They finally called off the concert. / They finally called the concert off.

The company laid off his whole group of friends in September. / The company laid his whole group of friends off in September.

If the object is a personal pronoun (as in the title sentence), it always goes inside the phrasal verb:

> It can be difficult to tell them apart [*Not:* It can be difficult to tell apart them.]
> They finally called it off. [*Not:* They finally called off it.]
> The company laid them off in September. [*Not:* The company laid off them in September.]

There is no rule about which transitive phrasal verbs can be separated and which cannot; they must be memorized individually or looked up in a dictionary.

Three-word phrasal verbs can never be separated:

> He's finally come up with an answer. [*Not:* He's finally come up an answer with.]
> They stole some TV sets and got away with it. [*Not:* They stole some TV sets and got it away with.]
> She's cutting down on carbohydrates. [*Not:* She's cutting down carbohydrates on.]

And phrasal verbs in the passive voice are never separated:

> They've been held up in traffic. [*Not:* They've been held in traffic up.]
> That year he was laid off by the factory. [*Not:* That year he was laid by the factory off.]

✔ Check

1. Find the Phrasal Verbs

Underline the phrasal verbs in the sentences below. Some of them may be separated.

Examples: He <u>called in</u> the reinforcements.
            She <u>held</u> her jealous boyfriend <u>back</u>.

1. I am waiting to set up the projector.

2. We settled in for the night.

3. She decided to call in.

4. The dog barked at me until the owner called it off.

5. I hope I can get my point across.

6. The people were just going about their business.

7. When I whistled, the horse's ears perked up.

8. He backed away from the edge of the cliff.

9. What subject are you going to take up in college?

10. Hold on, I'm coming!

2. Transitive or Intransitive?

Using the sentences in exercise 1, write whether the phrasal verb is transitive or intransitive.

Example: He called in the reinforcements. <u>transitive</u>
She held her jealous boyfriend back. <u>transitive</u>

1. I am waiting to set up the projector. _____

2. We settled in for the night. _____

3. She decided to call in. _____

4. The dog barked at me until the owner called it off. _____

5. I hope I can get my point across. _____

6. The people were just going about their business. _____

7. When I whistled, the horse's ears perked up. _____

8. He backed away from the edge of the cliff. _____

9. What subject are you going to take up in college? _____

10. Hold on, I'm coming! _____

41 I came here ~~for~~ to learn English.

In the sentence above, "to learn" is called an *infinitive of purpose,* because it says why someone did something.

>   She's moving east to be close to her daughter.
>   He bought the farm to grow corn.

In order to or *so as to* can be used instead of just *to:*

>   She's moving east so as to be close to her daughter.
>   He bought the farm in order to grow corn.

Or you can use *so* or *in order* followed by a *that*-clause:

>   She's moving east so that she can be close to her daughter.
>   He bought the farm in order that he could grow corn.

Or you can use *for,* followed by either a noun (or noun phrase) or an *–ing* form:

>   He moved there for his health. [= He moved there to improve his health.]
>   She keeps the dog for protection. [= She keeps the dog (in order) to have protection.]
>   I use this knife for chopping fruit. [= I use this knife (in order) to chop fruit.]
>   A barometer is used for measuring air pressure. [= A barometer is used to measure air pressure.]

Thus, *for* and *to* can both be used to express the same meaning, but "for to" (as in the title sentence) is never correct.

✓ Check

1. Combine the Sentences

Combine each pair of sentences by including an infinitive of purpose.

Example: He went to Florida. He saw his mother.
               → He went to Florida to see his mother.
               or He went to Florida so as to see his mother.
               or He went to Florida in order to see his mother.

1. He bought a camera. He takes photos of his dogs.

     _____

2. She went to college. She got a better job.

     _____

3. Cyclists should wear bright clothes. They make people more visible.

     _____

4. I go to the gym every day. I am getting fit.

     _____

5. My parents came here by bus. They saved money.

     _____

6. I went to the optometrist. I had my eyes tested.

     _____

7. He went into the house. He washed his hands.

     _____

8. She has gone upstairs. She is resting.

     _____

2. Rewrite with "So That"

Rewrite each sentence using "so that . . . can" or "so that . . . could."

Example: He went to Florida to see his mother.
                  → He went to Florida so that he could see his mother.

1. He wants to buy a boat to go sailing every weekend.

    _____

2. She wants to stop working to spend more time with her children.

    _____

3. Athletes train every day to keep fit.

    _____

4. I moved to the country to keep horses.

    _____

5. She studied hard to impress her professors.

    _____

42 I still miss my ~~father that~~ *father, who* I loved dearly.

A *relative clause* is a subordinate clause (a clause that can't stand by itself as a complete sentence) that describes or modifies a noun. Notice how the relative clause in each of the following sentences (shown in italics) describes the noun that it follows:

> This is the computer *that I want to buy.*
> The muscles *that hurt the most* are in my shoulders.
> The priest, *who was from Canada,* met us at the church gate.
> These two subjects, *which are closely related,* are the really important ones.

There are two kinds of relative clauses: *defining* (or *restrictive*) and *nondefining* (or *nonrestrictive*). A sentence with a defining clause needs the clause in order to make sense; a sentence with a nondefining clause doesn't actually need the clause in order to make sense. The first two of the four sentences above have defining clauses, and the last two have nondefining clauses. The first two sentences below are grammatically correct but don't contain all the information that they need:

> This is the computer.
> The muscles are in my shoulders.
> The priest met us at the church gate.
> These two subjects are the really important ones.

A relative clause generally begins with a relative pronoun, usually _that_, _which_, _who_, or _whom_. _Who_ and _whom_ only refer to people (and sometimes animals); _that_ refers to things and often to people and animals; _which_ refers to things but never to people. Nondefining clauses never begin with _that_.

Notice that clauses can be identified by their punctuation. A nondefining clause is separated from the rest of the sentence by commas; a defining clause is not.

> My house, which I bought in 2002, is now worth $250,000. [_Not:_ My house that I bought in 2002 is now worth $250,000.]
> Thieves stole her car, which she had parked in the wrong place. [_Not:_ Thieves stole her car that she had parked in the wrong place.]

Notice also that _that_ may only introduce defining clauses, but _which_ may introduce both defining and nondefining clauses.

> This is the computer which I want to buy.

That is often used in place of _who_ or _whom_, but _which_ never is.

> Those are the girls that [_or_ who _or_ whom] I want you to meet.
> The doctor that [_or_ who _or_ whom] we like best is Dr. Hall.

When a relative pronoun is the object of a defining clause, it can be omitted:

> That's the man [who _or_ whom _or_ that] I saw yesterday.
> The fruit [that _or_ which] they were served was extremely odd.
> She was the actress [who _or_ whom _or_ that] the playwright wrote the part for.

But the pronoun can never be omitted when it is the clause's subject:

> There's the man who caught the thief. [_Not:_ There's the man caught the thief.]

The mountain that overlooks the house is the steepest. [*Not:* The mountain overlooks the house is the steepest.]

See Unit 43 for more on relative clauses.

✔ Check

1. Fill in the Blanks

Fill in each blank with the correct relative pronoun. Some sentences may have more than one correct answer.

1. The lawyer _____ was in charge of our case met us at the courthouse.

2. The sisters, _____ went to school with my mother, arrived last night.

3. The man _____ you met yesterday is giving a speech here tonight.

4. My grandparents, _____ I never knew, lived in Kansas.

5. Norman, with _____ I had lunch, is the man in the blue sweater.

6. Those are my daughter's teachers, for _____ I have the greatest respect.

7. The blue whale, _____ is the largest creature that has ever lived, is an endangered species.

8. That is the table _____ my grandfather made.

9. I tried to learn a lot about the country _____ I was going to visit.

10. Max is the man _____ caught the thief.

2. Combine the Sentences

Combine the two sentences into one sentence containing a relative clause.

Example: My grandparents lived in Kansas. I never knew them.
       → My grandparents, whom I never knew, lived in Kansas.

1. The first singer was the best performer. He lived in Chicago.

    _____

2. The defendants were found guilty. They worked with my brother.

    _____

3. Maria is my best pupil. You have already met her.

    _____

4. My favorite painting is that one. I bought it in Spain.

    _____

5. The cheetah is a member of the cat family. It is the fastest land animal.

    _____

43 Last night is the time ~~it happened~~ then.

when it happened

A relative clause often starts with a word that isn't a relative pronoun. This is usually either a relative adverb—*when, where,* or *why*—or a relative adjective—*which* or *whose.*

> The climate is the reason why we moved to California.
> In 1848, when revolutions broke out across Europe, Marx published his *Communist Manifesto.*
> They had been to Mexico's Copper Canyon, where the Tarahumara Indians live.
> This is the man whose brother we met last night.
> My favorite uncle, whose jokes were funnier than anyone else's, gave great parties.
> It's not clear which road we're supposed to take.
> That was the year when he died. [*Or:* That was the year in which he died.]
> That's the house where I was born. [*Or:* That's the house in which I was born.]

Note that *when* and *where* can often be replaced by "in which" if the stated time or place ("the year," "the house," etc.) could have the word "in" in front of it.

When and *why* can often be omitted from a defining clause:

> The day [when] the festival was held was cloudy and cold.
> That's the main reason [why] the war lasted so long.

Where may also often be omitted, but only if a preposition is added:

> That's the town where I grew up. = That's the town I grew up in.

The verb in a relative clause must always agree in number with the noun or pronoun that is being modified. That is, both noun (or pronoun) and verb must be singular, or both must be plural:

> The land that they own is [*not* are] now very valuable.
> My brothers, who are [*not* is] very conservative, prefer the other candidate.
> The numbers in the document, which were checked by my assistant, are all accurate.

Note that the noun or pronoun that is modified is not always the last noun before the relative clause.

✓ Check

1. Fill in the Blanks

Complete each sentence using a relative adjective (*which* or *whose*) or relative adverb (*when*, *where*, or *why*).

1. Do you know _____ house is his?

2. We visited the mountains, _____ my uncle has a house.

3. That is _____ you are never supposed to walk alone at night.

4. The Metropolitan Opera, _____ Pavarotti gave his last opera performance, is in New York City.

5. That woman, _____ husband is the owner of the bank, shops on Rodeo Drive.

2. Insert the Missing Word

Insert the correct relative adverb (*when* or *why*) into each sentence in the proper place. (All the sentences are correct even without the adverb.)

Example: The day the festival was held was cloudy and cold.
       → The day *when* the festival was held was cloudy and cold.

1. During the year he was in the Navy, he was injured.

2. He is the reason I'm late.

3. The summer I went abroad was the best summer of my life.

4. That was the night their house burned down.

5. No one knew the reason she left.

44 He was right, ~~isn't it?~~ *wasn't he*

English conversation often makes use of *tag questions* (or *question tags*), little questions that are added to the end of ordinary sentences. They are also common in informal electronic messages, but they are rarely seen in other writing.

In some languages, a single tag question (which usually means "isn't it?") is used for all statements. But in English, every tag question is formed specially for the individual sentence.

If a statement is positive, the tag question must be negative. If a statement is negative, the tag question must be positive.

> It's hot today, isn't it?
> Churchill's mother was American, wasn't she?
> We can't go tomorrow, can we?
> Clare doesn't live here anymore, does she?

The tag question's subject is generally a personal pronoun: *I, you, he, she, it, we,* or *they*. But if the sentence starts with "There" ("There is," "There were," etc.), *there* is used in the tag question:

> There was a storm last night, wasn't there?
> There won't be any classes in January, will there?

The verb in the tag question is always an auxiliary verb: *be, have, do,* or a modal auxiliary. Usually the auxiliary has appeared in the main part of the sentence:

> John wouldn't leave her there alone, would he?
> You didn't go out last night, did you?
> Her sister will help us, won't she?

A form of *have* is used if the statement is in a perfect tense; a form of *be* is used if the statement is in a continuous tense:

> They have won all their games, haven't they?
> You've read *Hamlet*, haven't you?
> You hadn't been to Singapore before, had you?
> They had already made their decision, hadn't they?
> She's coming soon, isn't she?
> The children were having fun, weren't they?

However, a form of *do* is used in tag questions even when it doesn't appear earlier. *Do* is used whenever the statement is in the simple present or simple past. The only exception is when *be* is the main verb in the sentence.

> It still runs, doesn't it?
> He loves her, doesn't he?
> You liked the show, didn't you?
> It never snows here, does it?
> They won all their games, didn't they?
> We're late, aren't we?
> It wasn't exactly our best vacation, was it?

Often a tag question isn't really a question, but just a pleasant way to get the person you're addressing to respond. In such cases, your voice should usually go down at the end, not up:

> You're Wendy, aren't you? (↓)
> The weather's beautiful today, isn't it? (↓)

But when it is intended as a genuine question, your voice should go up. For example, if you're not sure that a friend can drive, you may say:

> You *can* drive, can't you? (↑)

Or if you see someone who you thought was French having difficulty reading a French sign, you may say:

> You *are* French, aren't you? (↑)

And the person may reply, for example, "No, I'm Portuguese," or "Yes, but I don't have my glasses with me."

One tag question has an unusual verb form: After a positive sentence beginning "I am," the tag question "aren't I?" is used (rather than "am I not," which sounds old-fashioned). But "am I?" is used after "I'm not," as you would expect.

> I'm winning, aren't I?
> I'm not boring you, am I?

Since most tag questions aren't really questions at all, but are instead just ways of bringing the listener into the conversation, you don't need to use them in your own conversations. But if you do, your English will sound more natural and friendly.

✔ Check —————————————————————

1. Fill in the Blanks

Fill in the blanks in these sentences.

1. Arthur isn't very busy, _____ he?

2. It isn't working, _____ _____?

3. Jennifer teaches your son, _____ she?

4. The news _____ very depressing, _____ it?

5. Bob _____ like me very much, does _____?

6. Alice and Dave had seen the movie before, _____ _____?

7. I'm older than your sister, _____ I?

8. You can play the piano, _____ _____?

9. His wife will be with him, _____ _____?

10. Your son has finished his exams now, _____ _____?

11. You didn't offer her the job, _____ _____ ?

12. They drove here, _____ _____?

13. We loved the play, _____ _____?

14. It _____ worry us, does it?

15. It's cooler on the beach, _____ _____?

2. Add the Right Tag

Add the correct tag question to each statement.

Examples: It's hot today.
      → It's hot today, isn't it?
      Andrew didn't go to the party.
      → Andrew didn't go to the party, did he?

1. Elizabeth doesn't work here, _____?

2. Charles knows her, _____?

3. I'm taller than your brother, _____?

4. It doesn't open until nine o'clock, _____?

5. It isn't snowing, _____?

6. Mary and Jack wouldn't like it here, _____?

7. Christine isn't happy, _____?

8. I'm talking too much, _____?

9. Your brother will be at the party, _____?

10. The weather's awful at the moment, _____?

11. They arrived here last week, _____?

12. It's cold in here, _____?

13. They had met before, _____?

14. Your daughter has learned how to swim, _____?

15. We enjoyed the meal last night, _____?

45 It's there are
There is dark, but it is some stores that are still open.

To state that something simply exists, we often begin a sentence or clause with "There":

> There's an old lady living in the apartment above mine. [= An old lady lives in the apartment above mine.]
> There are some Algerian boys in our class. [= Some Algerian boys are in our class.]

"There" is also sometimes used to state that something happened, often suddenly:

> There was a burst of applause from the audience. [= The audience produced a burst of applause.]

In a clause or sentence that follows the *there*-clause or *there*-sentence, we usually use *he*, *she*, *it*, *they*, or a relative pronoun:

> There's an old lady living in the apartment above mine. She gets up early.
> There are some Algerian boys in our class, and they are all related to each other.
> There was a burst of applause, which lasted almost a minute.

It is often used in a way similar to *there*—that is, to begin a sentence or clause without referring to a specific noun subject, often because there is no subject. *It* is used when stating the time or date, the weather or temperature, or a distance:

> It's only 9:00 a.m.
> It's already June and we haven't planted the garden.
> It's cold and wet there all winter.
> It's another twenty miles to the border.

It is also used to refer to a known fact or situation, or to something that is stated later in the sentence:

> It's healthy to eat fruit and grains. [= Eating fruit and grains is healthy.]
> It would be best to check your work one more time. [= You should check your work one more time.]
> If the airline goes bankrupt, it will be a disaster. [= The airline's bankruptcy would be a disaster.]
> It would be terrible if we lost. [= Losing would be terrible.]

Indefinite adjectives such as *all, a lot of, any, lots, more,* and *some* can come before either a plural count noun or a noncount noun. When one comes before a plural count noun (as in the title sentence), use "there are"; when it comes before a noncount noun, use "there is."

> There are a lot of small houses nearby.
> There's a lot of noise coming from the nightclub.

In negative sentences, use "there isn't" and "there aren't":

> There isn't much petroleum left in that region.
> There aren't any female managers in my company.
> Isn't there a bank nearby?
> Aren't there crocodiles in these rivers?

For past, present, and future tenses involving these uses of *it* and *there*, the verb form changes:

> There were 5,000 people at the concert.
> It was 85 degrees in the shade.
> There have been several recent earthquakes in California.
> It has been cold all week.
> There will be trouble when he learns the truth.
> It will be a ten-mile hike.

There and *it* are often used with modal verbs:

> There must be a gas station somewhere nearby.
> It must be 90 degrees out here.
> Will there be a storm this afternoon?
> It will be cold there in November.
> There could be a disaster if we're not careful.
> It could be another 20 miles.

Note that *there* and *it* can never simply be omitted, as they are in some other languages:

> There are 16 ounces in a pound. [*Not:* Are 16 ounces in a pound.]
> It's thirty miles to the river. [*Not:* Is thirty miles to the river.]

45 : <u>There is</u> ^{It's} dark, but <u>it is</u> ^{there are} some stores that are still open.

✓ Check ——————————————————

1. Fill in the Blanks

Fill in each blank with either *There* or *It* and the correct tense of *be*.

1. _____ a new student in the class.

2. _____ some flies in the kitchen.

3. _____ a good thing that you didn't get hurt.

4. _____ three miles to the next gas station.

5. _____ not a lot of cherries left on the tree.

6. _____ exciting when he finally gets here. (future tense)

7. _____ a grocery store nearby?

8. _____ an intermission during the play tonight? (future tense)

9. _____ a huge flood in Bangladesh yesterday.

10. _____ ten minutes left before the end of the class.

2. Make Sentences

Match up each beginning on the left with an ending on the right to complete a sentence.

1. There is   about 300 million people living in the U.S.

2. There are   raining by the time we get there—look at those thunderclouds!

3. There could be   some strong winds tonight if the storm blows in.

4. There isn't   that she left already and that's why the door is locked.

5. It is   some pizza left in the refrigerator?

6. It was   snowing in the mountains right now.

7. It could be   no smoke without fire.

8. It will be   any good restaurants near here?

9. Is there   any hope of a snowy Christmas this year because it has been so warm.

10. Are there   almost midnight before she arrived.

46 The place where I work
The place ~~where I work~~ there is one hour away.

A relative clause (see Units 42 and 43) usually begins with a relative pronoun or a relative adverb. When a relative pronoun (*who, whom, whose, which, that*) is the object of a verb or preposition, we never use another word with the same function later in the clause:

> The dog ran after the car that we were riding in. [*Not:* The dog ran after the car that we were riding in it.]
> I know who it belongs to. [*Not:* I know who it belongs to him.]

Similarly, when a relative adverb (*when, where, why*) begins a clause, another adverb must not repeat its function:

> The place where I work is five miles from my apartment. [*Not:* The place where I work there is five miles from my apartment.]
> We took them to a restaurant when they came to visit. [*Not:* We took them to a restaurant when they came to visit then.]

A relative pronoun in a defining clause can be omitted when it is the object of a verb or preposition, but not when it is the subject of a verb:

> My dad still owns the car [that] he bought in high school.
> The suit [which] he was married in was his cousin's.
> The people who own this house must be rich. [*Not:* The people own this house must be rich.]

Relative adverbs are never objects; however, a relative adverb in the middle (rather than the beginning) of a sentence can often be omitted:

> The office is the place [where] you spend most of your life.
> There are times [when] I regret my decision.

Even in sentences without a relative clause, English usually does not allow a noun function to be repeated by a pronoun. This is so even when a word group comes between the subject and verb.

> Life is beautiful. [*Not:* Life, it is beautiful.]
> The doctor advised me to quit smoking. [*Not:* The doctor he advised me to quit smoking.]

The story in the newspapers may be false. [*Not:* The story in the newspapers it may be false.]

The girls who had been crying were now laughing. [*Not:* The girls who had been crying they were now laughing.]

✔ Check

1. Delete the Pronoun or Adverb

Cross out any pronoun or adverb that incorrectly repeats the function of earlier words.

1. It is the doctor who he often suggests a new brand of drug.

2. Tonsillitis is one condition that it is curable.

3. Everyone needs friends who they are loyal.

4. The window, which is now clean, it reflects the sun.

5. Places where it is quiet and peaceful they are rare.

6. That winter especially was the time when he was working hard then.

7. Tom, my brother, he never misses the basketball games on TV.

8. I know the lady whose dog it is wearing a jacket.

9. He believes that you are what that you eat.

10. Sharon didn't say why the package it should not be opened.

2. Fill in the Blanks

Supply a pronoun or adverb if one is missing.

1. We tried to call the same manager we had spoken to _____ earlier.

2. The bulbs that she planted _____ will bloom beautifully next spring.

3. Our new teacher, _____ we saw on TV this morning, seems very nice.

4. This sculpture, _____ is new, is my favorite.

5. Why they spent so much money on a carpet _____ is a mystery to me.

47 I cut ~~my~~ hair at the hairdresser's on West Street.

have my hair cut

To talk about someone doing a job at the request of another person, you may use *have* followed by a noun phrase (such as "my hair") and a past participle (such as "cut"):

> I don't cut my hair myself; I have it cut [*or* done] at the hairdresser's.
> She doesn't service her car herself; she has it serviced [*or* done] at a garage.
> We don't clean our suits ourselves; we have them cleaned [*or* done] downtown.

Notice that the first clauses in these sentences use a *—self* or *—selves* word. They could instead have used the adjective *own:*

> I don't cut my own hair. I have it cut at the hairdresser's.

Get is just as common as *have* in such expressions, but slightly informal.

> You must get your hair cut before the wedding.
> I'll get my eyes tested this week.

The *have* and *get* expressions may appear in any tense:

> I had my camera fixed last week.
> They would get their house painted every three years if they could.
> He had had his suit cleaned twice that year already.

When the person or thing doing something is named, the verb that follows is in the infinitive, not the past participle:

> She'll have a brochure sent to you. → She'll have the company send you a brochure.
> They had their boat repaired last fall. → They had Mike repair their boat last fall.

135

47 : I ~~cut my hair~~ *have my hair cut* at the hairdresser's on West Street.

✓ Check

1. Answer the Questions

Use the word in parentheses to answer each question negatively, as in the example.

Example: Do you cut your hair yourself? (hairdresser)
             → No, I have it cut at the hairdresser's

1. Do you service your car yourself? (garage)

   _____

2. Do you do your own nails? (salon)

   _____

3. Does she dye her hair herself? (hairdresser)

   _____

4. Did you paint your house yourself? (house painters)

   _____

5. Did Peter design the garden himself? (gardener)

   _____

2. Can You Remember?

Mrs. Jones is about to have her daughter's wedding at her house. List the things that she "should have" done before the wedding day, as in the example.

Example: The carpets are dirty.
             → She should have the carpets cleaned.

1. The curtains are dirty.

   _____

2. The lock on the front gate is broken.

   _____

3. Her nails need to be done.

   _____

4. The cars need servicing.

    _____

5. The outside of the house needs painting.

    _____

6. The basement window needs to be replaced.

    _____

7. Her grass is too long.

    _____

8. The bathroom wallpaper is peeling.

    _____

9. The chimneys are filthy.

    _____

10. The basement is not decorated.

    _____

48 You *mustn't* ~~don't have to~~ be so polite.

L earners often use *must* incorrectly in negative sentences.

David has just started a new job, and his boss is telling him about it. The boss's positive statements may use either *must* or *have to*:

> You must [*or* have to] be here at nine o'clock every morning. You must [*or* have to] wear a tie.

Both *must* and *have to* are used for both present and future actions:

> You must [*or* have to] clean the office every evening.
> You must [*or* have to] be here on February 24th.

But *must* (like most modal verbs) lacks a past-tense form and cannot follow an auxiliary verb such as *have* or *will*. So for some tenses, only *have to* can be used:

> I had to clean the office before I went home.
> If the company moved to New York, I would have to find another job.
> If the company moves to New York, I will have to find another job.
> Since he lost his job, he has had to stop spending so much.

Must and *have to* mean the same thing in positive sentences, but not in negative sentences. David's new boss might say:

> You must [*or* have to] be here at eight o'clock, because someone has to [*or* must] turn on all the machines. You must [*or* have to] be on time. You must not be late.

The first two sentences are positive, so either *must* or *have to* can be used. But the third sentence is negative; if the boss had said "You don't have to be late," it would have meant "It isn't necessary for you to be late," which doesn't make sense.

But if the boss has six employees, he or she might say:

> One of you must [*or* has to] be here at eight o'clock. The rest of you don't have to be here until nine. [= The rest of you may come before nine, but you aren't required to.]

The first sentence is positive, so either *must* or *has to* is correct. But the second sentence is negative, so *must* and *have to* won't mean the same thing. If the boss had said "You must not be here until nine," it would have meant "You're not allowed to be here until nine."

Here are some final examples. On his first day at work, David wears his best suit:

> *Boss*: That's a nice suit, David. But you don't have to wear a suit for work if you don't want to.
> *David*: But I thought that we had to dress up for work.
> *Boss*: You must [*or* have to] wear a tie, but you don't have to wear a suit.

A week later, the boss speaks with David again:

> *Boss:* You're working too slowly. You must [*or* have to] work faster.
> *David*: I'm slow because I'm being careful.
> *Boss:* You don't have to be quite so careful. But you must not be so slow.

With a verb in the present perfect, *must* has a special meaning. You use it when you don't actually know if something has happened, but believe that it probably did:

> I must have left my glasses at home.
> She must have gone to the wrong address.
> There must have been a mistake.

✔ Check ————————————————

1. Fill in the Blanks

Fill in the blanks with *must* or *have to*. If both verbs would be correct, include them both.

1. You _____ sweep the floors before your friends can come over.

2. She does not _____ make a cake.

3. You don't _____ be here until 10:00.

4. I _____ finish the paper before I went home.

5. If she left the company, we would _____ hire a replacement.

6. You _____ be on time; you cannot be late.

7. If you want to pass your exams, you _____ work harder.

8. I _____ try to visit my parents more often.

9. You don't _____ have a passport to leave the state.

10. You usually _____ wait for hours before someone can see you.

2. *Must, Must Not,* or *Don't Have To?*

Fill in the blanks with *must, must not,* or *don't have to*. Each of these is used only once on each sign.

1. Sign on a beach

   a. You _____ wear a swimsuit.

   b. You _____ leave trash on the beach.

   c. You _____ swim when the lifeguard is absent.

139

49 : When I ~~go~~ come to stay with you, I will ~~take~~ bring it.

2. Sign in a restaurant kitchen

    a. You _____ touch the food with your bare hands.

    b. You _____ wear plastic gloves.

    c. You _____ work with any piece of equipment you are not familiar with.

3. Sign for shop clerks

    a. You _____ be rude.

    b. You _____ be helpful.

    c. You _____ say *sir* or *madam,* though the customer may think it is nice.

4. Sign on a restaurant door

    a. You _____ wear shoes.

    b. You _____ wear a jacket, but we would prefer it.

    c. You _____ bring pets into the restaurant.

5. On a vegetarian diet

    a. You _____ eat vegetables.

    b. You _____ eat mushrooms if you don't want to.

    c. You _____ eat meat.

49 When I ~~go~~ come to stay with you, I will ~~take~~ bring it.

In this unit we will look at two pairs of verbs that learners sometimes confuse: *come/go* and *bring/take.*

Both *come* and *go* mean "to travel," but they suggest two different directions of travel. You use *come* to talk about someone moving toward you or toward your listener. That is, the two of you may use the same word even if you are far apart. But you generally use *go* if the travel is in a direction away from both of you.

In the following telephone conversation, Tom, who is in New York, is speaking to Jane, who is in Chicago.

> *Tom:* Are you coming to New York this weekend?
>
> *Jane:* No, I can't come this weekend, because my sister is coming to stay with me. I can come to New York next weekend.
>
> *Tom:* I'm sorry, I won't be here then: I'm going to London. What about the following weekend?
>
> *Jane:* I can't come to New York then, because I'm going to Washington.

For *bring* and *take*, direction is also important. *Bring* is often used with *come*, and *take* is often used with *go:*

> When you come to see me, be sure to bring your mother.
> Whenever we go abroad, we always take our passports.

However, you will often hear native English-speakers use *bring* instead of *take* in a sentence like the last one.

✔ Check

1. Making Conversations

Bill, Tom, and Dan are fixing a roof. Dan is on the ground, and Bill and Tom are on the roof. Fill in each blank in the conversation below with the correct verb.

> *Bill:* Dan, would you _____ us a hammer?
>
> *Dan:* I'll _____ it up when I _____ up the ladder.
>
> *Tom*: When will you _____ up here?
>
> *Dan:* When I'm finished unloading the roofing materials. Do you need me to _____ anything else?
>
> *Tom:* If you'd _____ me some water, that would be great.
>
> *Bill:* And if you could _____ this crowbar and put it back in the truck, I'd appreciate it.
>
> *Dan:* I'll _____ you the hammer and some water and then _____ the crowbar back to the truck, then.

2. Choose the Right Verb

Read this telephone conversation between Laura, who is in Los Angeles, and Stefan, who is in San Francisco, and underline the correct verbs.

Stefan: Are you (1) coming/going to San Francisco this weekend?

Laura: No, I can't (2) come/go this weekend because I'm (3) coming/going to Paris. I can (4) come/go to San Francisco next weekend.

Stefan: I'm sorry, I won't be here then: I'm (5) coming/going to Seattle. What about the weekend after?

Laura: I can't (6) come/go to San Francisco then, because my mother is (7) coming/going to Los Angeles to stay with me.

Stefan: Can you (8) come/go here for Thanksgiving?

Laura: Yes, I can (9) come/go then, because my mother is (10) coming/going back to New York two days before Thanksgiving.

50 I am used to ~~drive~~ *driving* on the right, not the left.

The expression *be used to* means "be accustomed to." It is always followed by a noun or a gerund (*-ing* form):

Are the summers in New York too hot for you?

- No. I was brought up in Africa, so I'm used to hot weather. And I'm used to living in an apartment. But I'm not used to so much traffic!

Get used to means "get accustomed to." Like *be used to*, *get used to* is generally followed by a noun or an *–ing* form:

I'm getting used to driving on the left side of the road, but I'll never get used to the speed of life in New York.

The phrase "can't get used to" can be useful:

I'm used to most things about American life now, but I still can't get used to the way people dress.

Don't confuse *be used to* or *get used to* with the auxiliary *used to*, which refers to a continuing situation or frequent action in the past that is now finished (see Unit 28):

I am used to riding a bicycle in a big city. When I lived in Amsterdam, I used to ride a bicycle all the time.

✓ Check

1. Rewrite

Rewrite the sentences using the correct form of *be used to*.

Example: I moved to New York just two weeks ago.
              → I'm not used to living in New York.

1. I have been wearing heels for just two days.

   _____

2. She has just got an office job for the first time.

   _____

3. They have problems with American money.

   _____

4. I've been speaking English for many years, so it isn't a problem.

   _____

5. I usually get up late, but now I have to get up early and it is difficult.

   _____

2. Which *Used To?*

In the blank after each sentence, write either "auxiliary" (if "used to" expresses a continuing situation or frequent action in the past) or "adjective" (if "used to" means "accustomed to").

1. We used to go to the movies all the time. _____

2. I can't get used to traveling so much. _____

3. Are you used to the sun here? _____

4. When I lived in South America, I used to hike all the time. _____

5. I used to go swimming in a pool, but I'm still not used to swimming in the ocean.

   _____

Reference Section *1*

The Tenses of English

Simple present

Form

The simple present is formed with the infinitive form of the verb, except in the third-person singular.

Positive	Negative	Questions
I/you/we/they work	I/you/we/they do not work	Do I/you/we/they work?
he/she/it works	he/she/it does not work	Does he/she/it work?

Use

1. The simple present is used to talk about habitual actions and things that happen regularly.

    I get up at seven o'clock every day.

2. It is also used to express general truths and timeless actions.

    Water boils at 100° C.

3. It is not often used to describe an actual action that is happening now.

Present continuous

Form

The present continuous is formed with *be* and the present participle (-*ing* form) of the verb.

Positive	Negative	Questions
I am working	I am not working	Am I working?
you/we/they are working	you/we/they are not working	Are you/we/they working?
he/she/it is working	he/she/it is not working	Is he/she/it working?

Use

1. The present continuous is used to describe an event that is happening now.

    The team is coming onto the field now.

2. It is used to talk about something that is continuing to happen.

    He's studying to become a priest.

3. It is often used informally to talk about something that will happen in the near future.

    I'm seeing her next week.

Present perfect

Form

The present perfect is formed with *have/has* and the past participle.

Positive	Negative	Questions
I/you/we/they have seen	I/you/we/they have not seen	Have I/you/we/they seen?
he/she/it has seen	he/she/it has not seen	Has he/she/it seen?

Use

1. The present perfect is used to describe past actions when the time frame hasn't finished.

    We have visited seven countries.
    She hasn't been back in many years.
    The treaty has been in effect since 1998.

    (By contrast, the simple past tense is used when the time frame is finished: "In 1994 I visited three countries," or "I didn't do much when I was young.")

2. It is used to describe a past action when the time of the action is vague or not important.

    I've already read that book.
    He has thought about going back to school.

3. It is used to describe an event that happened very recently and therefore affects the present.

> They've lost the briefcase.
> She has broken her arm.

Present perfect continuous

Form

The present perfect continuous is formed with *have/has been* and the present participle (*–ing* form) of the verb.

Positive	Negative	Questions
I/you/we/they have been doing	I/you/we/they have not been doing	Have I/you/we/they been doing?
he/she/it has been doing	he/she/it has not been doing	Has he/she/it been doing?

Use

1. The present perfect continuous describes an action or state that started in the past and still exists or is still happening now.

> I've been waiting here for five hours. [= I came here five hours ago, and I am still waiting here now.]

2. It is also used to describe a regular or habitual action from the past that continues into the present.

> I've been playing tennis lately.
> He's been going to nightclubs a lot this summer.

Simple past

Form

The simple past is normally formed by adding *–ed* to the end of the verb.

Positive	Negative	Questions
I/you/he/she/it/we/they worked	I/you/he/she/it/we/they did not work	Did I/you/he/she/it/we/they work?

If the verb ends with a consonant + -*y*, the *y* changes to *i (study / studied)*. If the verb ends in -*e*, -*d* rather than -*ed* is added *(live / lived)*. If the verb ends in a single vowel and consonant, and the last (or only) syllable is stressed, the consonant is doubled *(quiz / quizzed)*. Many verbs are irregular in the past tense; see the list of irregular verbs on p. 150.

Use

1. The simple past is used to talk about events that happened in the past.

    They left quietly before dawn.
    In 1812 he attempted to invade Russia.

2. It is used to talk about continuing states or regular actions that existed or were done in the past.

    It was a terrible time for them.
    She always talked about her father fondly.

Past continuous

Form

The past continuous is formed with *was/were* and the present participle (–*ing* form) of the verb.

Positive	Negative	Questions
I/he/she/it was playing	I/he/she/it was not playing	Was I/he/she/it playing?
You/we/they were playing	You/we/they were not playing	Were you/we/they playing?

Use

1. The past continuous is used for a past action that hadn't finished at a particular time.

    At six o'clock we were still working.

2. It is used to speak about an action or state that continued at the same time as another action or state, or an action that had not finished when some event occurred. It is often used in a clause beginning with *while, as,* or *when;* the event clause usually uses the simple past and often begins with *when.*

While we were working, he was playing tennis.
While she was taking a bath, the phone rang.
When the phone rang, she was taking a bath.
As we were talking, a strange thing happened.
I saw the play when/while I was living in New York.

Past perfect

Form

The past perfect is formed with *had* and the past participle.

Positive	Negative	Questions
I/you/he/she/it/we/they had arrived	I/you/he/she/it/we/they had not arrived	Had I/you/he/she/it/we/they arrived?

Use

1. The past perfect is used to talk about an action that was completed before another past action or past time. The simple past is usually used for the other action or time.

    Before the first wheels were made from metal in 1813, people had used wood.
    I had never met a Bulgarian until I met her.

    The clause with the other verb can be omitted when it is clear what other action or time is being referred to.

    She had seen the house only once.
    They hadn't known.

2. It is used in an *if*-clause to talk about a possible past action that didn't occur.

    If I had known that, I wouldn't have sent the letter.

Simple future

Form

The simple future is formed with either *will* or, less formally, *be going to*, followed by the infinitive form of the verb. (*Shall* is sometimes used in place of *will* in the first person.)

Positive	Negative	Questions
I/you/he/she/it/we/they will sing	I/you/he/she/it/we/they will not sing	Will I/you/he/she/it/we/they sing?

Positive	Negative	Questions
I am going to sing	I am not going to sing	Am I going to sing?
you/we/they are going to sing	you/we/they are not going to sing	Are you/we/they going to sing?
he/she/it is going to sing	he/she/it is not going to sing	Is he/she/it going to sing?

Use

1. The simple future is used to express a prediction about the future.

   Life in the next century will be easier.
   She's sure everything is going to be fine.

2. It is used informally to express an intention.

   That's the doorbell—I'll answer it.
   I'm going to write to her.

3. It is used in a result clause following an *if*-clause when the result is likely.

   If I'm right, the company will suffer.
   If he doesn't hurry, he is going to miss the bus.

Future Continuous

Form

The future continuous uses *will be* or, less formally, *be going to be* and the present participle (*–ing* form) of the main verb.

Positive	Negative	Questions
I/you/he/she/it/we/they will be leaving	I/you/he/she/it/we/they will not be leaving	Will I/you/he/she/it/we/they be leaving?

Positive	Negative	Questions
I am going to be leaving	I am not going to be leaving	Will I/you/he/she/it/we/they be leaving?
you/we/they are going to be leaving	you/we/they are not going to be leaving	
he/she/it is going to be leaving	he/she/it is not going to be leaving	

Use

1. The future continuous is used informally exactly like the simple future tense, to describe events (both continuing actions and single events) that will occur sometime in the future.

> He's going to be working in the woods tomorrow.
> We'll be leaving soon; it's almost midnight.

2. It is used to express an action that will continue from the present into the future.

> They'll still be arguing about it when we get back.

Future perfect

Form

The future perfect is formed with *will have* and the past participle.

Positive	Negative	Questions
I/you/he/she/it/we/they will have worked	I/you/he/she/it/we/they will not have worked	Will I/you/he/she/it/we/they have worked?

Use

1. The future perfect is used—often with *by, by the time,* or *when*—for a future action that will be finished before a specified future time.

> By six o'clock we will have finished the job.
> She will have had the baby by the next time I see her.
> When you come, they will have already bought a new house.

It does not appear in clauses introduced by "time words" such as "before" and "by the time," where the present perfect is used instead ("She will have finished her job long before he has done his," "I will lend you the novel as soon as I have read it," "The meal will be ready by the time you've had your drinks").

Reference Section *2*

Common Irregular Verbs

The list below shows all the common verbs that are always or sometimes irregular.

Infinitive	Past Tense	Past Participle	Infinitive	Past Tense	Past Participle
be	was/were	been	creep	crept	crept
bear	bore	borne	cut	cut	cut
beat	beat	beaten *or* beat	deal	dealt	dealt
			dig	dug	dug
become	became	become	do	did	done
begin	began	begun	draw	drew	drawn
bend	bent	bent	dream	dreamed *or* dreamt	dreamed *or* dreamt
bet	bet	bet			
bid	bade *or* bid	bidden *or* bid	drink	drank	drunk
bind	bound	bound	drive	drove	driven
bite	bit	bitten	eat	ate	eaten
bleed	bled	bled	fall	fell	fallen
blow	blew	blown	feed	fed	fed
break	broke	broken	feel	felt	felt
breed	bred	bred	fight	fought	fought
bring	brought	brought	find	found	found
broadcast	broadcast	broadcast	flee	fled	fled
build	built	built	fly	flew	flown
burn	burned *or* burnt	burned *or* burnt	forbid	forbade *or* forbad	forbidden
burst	burst *or* bursted	burst *or* bursted	forget	forgot	forgotten *or* forgot
buy	bought	bought	forgive	forgave	forgiven
can	could	—	freeze	froze	frozen
catch	caught	caught	get	got	got *or* gotten
choose	chose	chosen	give	gave	given
cling	clung	clung	go	went	gone
come	came	come	grow	grew	grown
cost	cost	cost *or* costed	hang	hung	hung
could	—	—	have	had	had

Infinitive	Past Tense	Past Participle
hear	heard	heard
hide	hid	hidden *or* hid
hit	hit	hit
hold	held	held
hurt	hurt	hurt
keep	kept	kept
kneel	knelt	knelt
knit	knit *or* knitted	knit *or* knitted
know	knew	known
lay	laid	laid
lead	led	led
lean	leaned *or* leant	leaned *or* leant
learn	learned *or* learnt	learned *or* learnt
leave	left	left
lend	lent	lent
let	let	let
lie	lay	lain
light	lighted *or* lit	lighted *or* lit
lose	lost	lost
make	made	made
may	—	—
mean	meant	meant
meet	met	met
might	—	—
must	—	—
ought	—	—
pay	paid	paid
prove	proved	proved *or* proven
put	put	put
quit	quit	quit
read	read	read
ride	rode	ridden
ring	rang	rung
rise	rose	risen

Infinitive	Past Tense	Past Participle
run	ran	run
say	said	said
see	saw	seen
seek	sought	sought
sell	sold	sold
send	sent	sent
set	set	set
sew	sewed	sewn *or* sewed
shake	shook	shaken
shall	should	—
shine	shone *or* shined	shone *or* shined
shoot	shot	shot
should	—	—
show	showed	shown *or* showed
shrink	shrank *or* shrunk	shrunk *or* shrunken
shut	shut	shut
sing	sang *or* sung	sung
sink	sank *or* sunk	sunk
sit	sat	sat
sleep	slept	slept
slide	slid	slid
smell	smelled *or* smelt	smelled *or* smelt
sneak	sneaked *or* snuck	sneaked *or* snuck
speak	spoke	spoken
spend	spent	spent
spin	spun	spun
split	split	split
spread	spread	spread
stand	stood	stood
steal	stole	stolen
stick	stuck	stuck
sting	stung	stung

Infinitive	Past Tense	Past Participle	Infinitive	Past Tense	Past Participle
stink	stank	stunk	throw	threw	thrown
strike	struck	struck	understand	understood	understood
swear	swore	sworn	wake	woke	woken *or* waked
sweep	swept	swept			
swell	swelled	swelled *or* swollen	wear	wore	worn
			weave	wove *or* weaved	woven *or* weaved
swim	swam	swum			
swing	swung	swung	will	would	—
take	took	taken	win	won	won
teach	taught	taught	wind	wound	wound
tear	tore	torn	would	—	—
tell	told	told	write	wrote	written
think	thought	thought			

Answer Key

Unit 1

1.

1.	hotels	6.	zeros
2.	calves	7.	houses
3.	monkeys	8.	children
4.	echoes	9.	cows
5.	roofs	10.	sheep

2.

1. Chicken soup is one of my favorite dishes.
2. We heard the wolves howling at the moon.
3. Most of the houses in this town have red roofs.
4. I have autographs from all my soccer heroes.
5. We drove by three churches.
6. A flock of geese rested by the pond.
7. No one saw the thieves leave the house.
8. Remember to put the knives and forks by the plates.
9. She's terrified of rats and mice.
10. I saw the deer and their babies at the park!

3.

1. There are deer in the field.
2. The stores had pianos in their windows.
3. Please put the glasses on the shelves.
4. The women know the men.
5. The babies already have teeth.
6. She showed me photos of sheep.
7. Let's read (the) stories about (the) rabbits.
8. The girls are buying scarves.
9. Let the children eat them.
10. The tomatoes are in (the) bags, but the potatoes are in (the) boxes.

Unit 2

1. Those glasses suit you.
2. The news was bad. It upset him very much.
3. These pajamas are nice, and they are comfortable too.
4. All this furniture is beautiful, and it is all for sale.
5. Those scissors are dull; they need sharpening.
6. The information that you need is in this envelope.
7. My shorts are old but I still like them.
8. This is an interesting piece of research.
9. Economics is based on mathematics.
10. Physics was Einstein's field of study.

Unit 3

1.

1.   He isn't at home and we haven't seen him for weeks.
2.   She doesn't know where they're hiding.
3.   I'm sure she's telling the truth, but I'll ask her again.
4.   He said he'd met Angela once before.
5.   This is John's car.
6.   That is the boy's coat.
7.   That's the dog's bowl.
8.   Those are my children's beds.
9.   He should be on the men's team!
10.   This is my parents' car.
11.   Those are the boys' bedrooms.
12.   It's been snowing for hours.
13.   Each dog has its own bowl.
14.   Every language has its own difficulties.
15.   He is coming in two weeks' time.
16.   I'd like a dollar's worth of nails please.
17.   Meet me at the station at one o'clock.
18.   There are two *l*'s in *hill*.
19.   Here's a list of do's and don't's.
20.   She grew up during the '60s [or '60's].

2.

1.   She's not at work and she hasn't been there for weeks.
2.   Those are the children's books.
3.   He bought twenty dollars' worth of nails.
4.   Is it six o'clock yet?
5.   You mustn't drive David's car.
6.   That's my child's toy.
7.   The girl's name is Charlotte Brown.
8.   Each house has its own mailbox.
9.   These are my sisters' bedrooms.
10.   You must give two weeks' notice if you're going to leave your job.

Unit 4

1.

1.   She came in and said, "We will be taking a short quiz this morning."
2.   I was standing near Bill Clinton during the press conference.
3.   Queen Elizabeth and President Sarkozy were invited to the event at the UN.
4.   I was happy to see my neighbor, Ms. Jones.
5.   We open our presents on Christmas Day, not Christmas Eve.
6.   I'm meeting John next Monday.
7.   The people of Canada are the Canadians. They speak English and French.
8.   My address is 100 Commonwealth Ave., Boston, Mass.
9.   We drove through Death Valley on our way to see the Grand Canyon.

10. She converted from Catholicism to Buddhism.
11. The U.S. Department of Defense is seeking more funding from Congress.
12. Did he fight in World War I or World War II?
13. She prefers to drink Stolichnaya when she can get it.
14. The movie *Clueless* was based on Jane Austen's novel *Emma*.
15. There is a long article in the Sunday *New York Times* about Beethoven and his works.

Unit 5

1.

1. She is a good friend.
2. She is a teacher.
3. He is an engineer.
4. It's an elephant.
5. This car can go 140 miles an hour.
6. This is an X-ray.
7. John is a cabdriver.
8. It's a European car.
9. What a beautiful painting!
10. I bought an orange and some bread.

2.

1. Jane Walker is a nurse.
2. She wears a uniform to work.
3. It takes her an hour to drive to work.
4. Her car is an MG, which is a European car.
5. Jane has two children: a two-year-old boy and an eleven-year-old girl.
6. She's such a busy woman!
7. For Jane the most important things in life are health and happiness.
8. Jane's husband, John, is an engineer.
9. He went to the hardware store and bought a hundred nails at twenty cents a dozen.
10. John's parents are both teachers.
11. John thinks that Jane is a good mother and a good wife.
12. Jane thinks that John is a good father and a good husband.

Unit 6

1.

1. This problem is important, but it's not a matter of life and death.
2. He never got over the death of his father.
3. There was a bright light in the sky.
4. George is in the garage.
5. At the end of the road, there was a house. The house looked empty.
6. That is the man who took my bag.
7. The Mississippi is the longest river in the U.S.
8. Amsterdam is the biggest city in the Netherlands.
9. We go to a/the local grocery store, but I like the store in the city much better.
10. His wife has been in the hospital for the last three weeks.

2.

1. I think that the most important things in life are health and happiness.
2. George never recovered from the loss of his business.
3. I have a red rose, a white rose, and a pink rose, but the red rose is the prettiest one.
4. That is the largest business in the city.
5. Amundsen was the first man to reach the South Pole.
6. Henry is in the garden and Lucy is in the bathroom.
7. The telephone is over there, on the television and next to the lamp.
8. The man in the black hat can give you all the information that you need.
9. The Rockies are not near New York; they are closer to the West Coast of the U.S.
10. The Seychelles are a group of islands in the Indian Ocean.
11. The Thames is the most famous river in England.
12. I know that bears hibernate, and I think that hedgehogs hibernate, too.
13. He leaves home at 7:00 in the morning, and he gets back to the house at 7:00 in the evening.
14. When they lived in the U.S., they went to church every Sunday.
15. He has four children: three girls and a boy. The oldest girl is in college, and the youngest girl is in school in Switzerland.

Unit 7

1.

1. There isn't anything in the fridge to eat.
2. I would like some fruit, please.
3. I want to eat something hot.
4. I'm not going anywhere today.
5. Do you have any questions?
6. I lost the key somewhere in the house.
7. Is anybody coming to our party? If not, we'll have to cancel it.
8. You're very pale. Is something/anything wrong?
9. We spoke to someone who looked like your brother.
10. I can't find any shoes that I like.

2.

1. I'd like some wine, but I don't want any cheese.
2. I don't want any rice, but I'd like some salad.
3. I'd like some bread, but I don't want any butter.
4. I'd like some ham, but I don't want any mustard.
5. I don't want any peas, but I'd like some potatoes.

3.

1. I need some coffee, but I don't need any tea.
2. There are some museums in this city, but there aren't any art galleries. *or*
   There are some museums in this city, but there are no art galleries.
3. We do have some jam, but we don't have any peanut butter.
4. There aren't any restaurants in this town, but there are some bars. *or*
   There are no restaurants in this town, but there are some bars.
5. There are some herbs in this dish, but there aren't any spices. *or*
   There are some herbs in this dish, but there are no spices.

6. There is no ginger in this dish, but there is some garlic. *or*
    There isn't any ginger in this dish, but there is some garlic.
7. I don't need any brownies, but I do need some cookies.
8. There isn't any milk in the fridge, but there is some orange juice. *or*
    There is no milk in the fridge, but there is some orange juice.
9. We do have some string in the shed, but we don't have any wire.
10. There are some Mexicans in the school, but there aren't any Brazilians. *or*
    There are some Mexicans in the school, but there are no Brazilians.

Unit 8

1.

1. How much coffee is there?
    Not much. There is plenty of / a lot of coffee.
2. How many tomatoes are there?
    Not many. There are plenty of / a lot of tomatoes.
3. How many men are there?
    Not many. There are plenty of / a lot of men.
4. How much water is there?
    Not much. There is plenty of / a lot of water.
5. How much flour is there?
    Not much. There is plenty of / a lot of flour.

2.

1. How many apples are there?
    There aren't many apples, but there are a lot of pears.
2. How much beef do we have?
    We have plenty of / a lot of beef, but we do not have much pork.
3. How many peas are there?
    There aren't many peas, but there are a lot of beans
4. How much pasta and rice is there?
    There is a lot of / plenty of pasta, but there is not much rice.
5. How many potatoes do we have?
    We don't have many potatoes, but we have plenty of / a lot of beets.

Unit 9

1.

1. Is there any tea? Yes, there is a little.
2. Are there any tomatoes? Yes, there are a few
3. Are there any children in the playground? Yes, there are a few.
4. Do we have any wine? Yes, we have a little.
5. Is there any rice left? Yes, there is a little left.

2.

1. I have little hope that he will be found.
2. There are fewer farms in the area than there were when I was young.
3. You'll find a gas station less than two miles from here.
4. Few women have achieved as much as she has.

5. Please give your answer in 50 words or less.
6. We've had less rain this spring than last spring.
7. There are fewer good restaurants in this town now.
8. I got a rental car, but I had little / less luck finding a hotel room.
9. There are a few good places to eat in town.
10. He had a few job offers to choose from.

Unit 10

1.

1. All / Both the drivers are over 21.
2. Every / Each driver is over 21.
3. The whole/entire class is under 18.
4. All (of) the streets in this part of town are closed.
5. The whole/entire store is under construction.
6. Each/Every state in the U.S. has two senators.
7. We reviewed each individual application very carefully.
8. All (of) the food is in that bag.
9. Each/Every one of our family members is important to us.
10. Each/Every piece of china had been carefully chosen.
11. His whole/entire hand was burned.
12. Both (of) the twins are good at basketball.
13. I gave candy to each of the three boys.
14. All of our four children want to go into medicine.
15. The movie lasted three whole hours!

2.

1. Every book in this shop is on sale.
2. All people in this town have the right to vote.
3. The whole family is invited.
4. Every chair needs to be replaced.
5. All (of) the houses on this street are different.
6. Every bottle has been recycled.
7. Each of his parents is very intelligent.
8. All of her leg is covered in mosquito bites.
9. Every team in the competition is European.
10. All (of) the plants in the garden need water.

Unit 11

1.

1. This class is quieter than that one.
2. This house is cleaner than that one.
3. This city is more important than that one.
4. This book is longer than that one.
5. This coat is more beautiful than that one.
6. This movie is more interesting than that one.
7. This child is happier than that one.
8. This carpet is thinner than that one.

9. This building is more modern than that one.
10. This painting is more expressive than that one.

2.

1. Blue flowers are more unusual than white ones.
2. Green peppers are tastier than red peppers.
3. Lions are more dangerous than house cats.
4. Jane is younger and fitter than her husband.
5. Tuesdays are better than Fridays for me.

3.

1. Easter is just as special as Christmas to me.
2. He thinks driving on the right is more difficult than driving on the left.
3. The bananas are selling for less money here than they are at that store.
4. Going by horse is not as quick as going by car.
5. The film is nowhere near as good as the book.
6. William is already as tall as his mother.
7. This class is far harder than the other class.
8. I am as trustworthy as she is.
9. This cake is not so good as the cake she made.
10. These exercises weren't nearly as hard as the previous ones.

Unit 12

1.

1. The Chrysler Building is the most unusual building in New York.
2. The Mona Lisa is the most famous painting in the Louvre.
3. Lisa is the tallest girl in our class.
4. Pelé is the most famous soccer player of all time.
5. We live on the quietest street in the town.
6. Albert Einstein was one of the most influential scientists ever.
7. It was the steepest mountain I had ever climbed.
8. This is the best cake.
9. She is the loveliest woman I've ever seen.
10. This one is the best of the lot.

Unit 13

1.

1. Do we have enough bread?
2. There aren't enough plumbers in Chicago.
3. Do you have enough large nails to do the job?
4. There is enough paint for all the students.
5. Those nails aren't large enough to do the job.
6. Is Harry strong enough to lift it?
7. I think my son is too fat.
8. Isn't it too cold to go swimming?
9. There are too many students in the class.
10. There aren't enough students in the class.

2.

1. Can we go to Australia for a vacation?
    No, the plane fare is too expensive.
2. Can I plant flowers here?
    No, the soil is too poor.
3. Can we solve the problem?
    No, we are not clever enough.
4. Can we take the table home?
    No, it is too heavy.
5. Can you buy this car?
    No, I am not rich enough.
6. Can we go in the swimming pool?
    No, the water is too cold.
7. Can we play on the lawn?
    No, the grass is too wet.
8. Can you carry that suitcase for me?
    No, I am not strong enough.
9. Will he apply for the job?
    No, he is not experienced enough.
10. Do you think she will go to the party?
    No, she is too busy.

3.

1. Is there enough water in the reservoir?
    Yes, there is enough water; in fact, there is too much.
2. Is there enough milk in the cake batter?
    Yes, there is enough milk; in fact, there is too much.
3. Are there enough books on the shelves?
    Yes, there are enough books; in fact, there are too many.
4. Are there enough chairs in the hall?
    Yes, there are enough chairs; in fact, there are too many.
5. Are there enough people in the lecture hall?
    Yes, there are enough people; in fact, there are too many.

Unit 14

1.

1. She was such a beautiful woman that everyone looked at her.
2. It was such an old car that no one bought it.
3. They are such naughty children that they can't be left alone.
4. It was such a long book that it took me a year to read it.
5. It is such a heavy package that mailing it will be too expensive.

2.

1. The weather was so bad that they canceled the parade.
2. He was so unpleasant that no one liked him.
3. The girl was so quiet that everyone ignored her.

4.   The storm was so bad that all the crops were ruined.

5.   The drawings are so rare that they're insured for $100,000.

Unit 15

1.

1.   The plan was beautifully simple.
2.   She was cruelly disappointed by his decision.
3.   He stated his opinion more confidently than his brother.
4.   I think this novel is the most imaginatively written of the three.
5.   They went up the stairs as quietly as they could.
6.   You can drive faster once we are out of the city.
7.   He hits the ball higher than most golfers.
8.   During gym class, she always jumped the highest and ran the fastest.
9.   She works very hard.
10.   Joanne plays piano quite well.
11.   She plays better than Alice.
12.   She is always the best prepared member of the orchestra.
13.   Mark drives badly.
14.   He drives even worse when he's tired.
15.   That car is the worst designed car that I have ever seen.

2.

1.   She sings beautifully.
2.   He learns quickly.
3.   They dance well.
4.   She describes things very clearly.
5.   They swim badly.
6.   We work hard.
7.   He runs faster than his brother.
8.   She speaks slower than her sister.
9.   He treated his dogs cruelly.
10.   He handled the negotiations smoothly.

Unit 16

1.

1.   It's a two-liter bottle.
2.   It's a three-man boat.
3.   She has a ten-inch-long tattoo on her back.
4.   We were followed by a long-haired man.
5.   I was introduced to a blue-eyed, fair-haired woman.

2.

1.   Octagons are shapes that have eight sides.
2.   Humans are creatures that have two legs.
3.   The turtle was eighty years old.
4.   The arrow that wounded him was two feet long.
5.   We need a team of twenty men.

Unit 17

1.

1. the ninth annual education conference
2. her two new dresses
3. some small yellow wooden tables
4. two enormous Chinese urns
5. an exotic, purple jungle flower

2.

1. She introduced us to three charming old Thai restaurants.
2. It was a large, ancient, yellow, Chinese gingko tree.
3. He was interested in a dirty, old, Arabian brass lamp.
4. They spent three long, cool summers in the mountains.
5. The college built a large, new, wooden student dormitory.

3.

1. his splendid, large, green, wooden
2. 45-year-old, slender, purple, glass
3. those two delightful British
4. All your dirty old Spanish gold
5. a small, antique, Japanese watering

Unit 18

1. The travel agent planned our entire vacation perfectly.
2. The story that they told us was extraordinarily moving.
3. We slowly drove along the icy mountain road. *or*
   We drove slowly along the icy mountain road. *or*
   We drove along the icy mountain road slowly.
4. He was seldom a better player than his cousin.
5. I felt especially tired this morning.

Unit 19

1.

1. You should have told your boss about it.
2. Did you think that you could have played better yesterday?
3. The bus might have left already.
4. She must have gone to the movie by herself.
5. They ought to have known that it was dangerous.

2.

1. Did you finish all that work yesterday?
2. I must complete this paper before next week.
3. Their children should do more work in the house.
4. We want to see the movie soon. *or* We can see the movie soon.
5. Should I go to my doctor?

Unit 20

1.

1. That bird flies very well.
2. He speaks English fluently.
3. They work hard and play hard.
4. How does she go to work?
5. She doesn't help her mother very much.
6. He eats and drinks too much.
7. Where do John and Louise live?
8. We want to help you.
9. In this country it rains all summer and snows all winter.
10. Mrs. Davis cooks all our meals and cleans the house.

2.

1. She prays in church every morning before she goes to work.
2. That blender buzzes loudly but it mixes well.
3. When she applies the paint to the wall, this paper catches the drips.
4. If you have the keys, please give them to me.
5. He is going to travel in Italy while his wife stays home.

Unit 21

1.

1. Daniel doesn't like white wine, but he sometimes drinks red wine.
2. He lives on Drury Lane.
3. Loud noises scare the children.
4. Emma works in a restaurant.
5. It is almost three o'clock.

2.

Ann: What are you doing now?
Tom: I am watching TV.
Ann: Is your wife watching TV?
Tom: No, she is not.
Ann: Is she reading a book?
Tom: No, she is not reading a book, she is writing a letter.

3.

1. Does Jane eat meat and fish?
   She sometimes eats meat, but she never eats fish.
2. Do Robert and Jim drink wine and beer?
   They sometimes drink wine, but they never drink beer.
3. Do you listen to pop music and jazz?
   I sometimes listen to pop music, but I never listen to jazz.

4.

1. Is David working?
   No, he's reading a book.
2. Are Lucy and Clare watching TV?
   No, they're listening to music.
3. Are you cutting the grass?
   No, I'm planting vegetables.

Unit 22

1.

1. They have already arrived.
2. Has it snowed here this week?
3. We have not stayed too long, I hope.
4. She hasn't told us what she wants.
5. I have watched three movies tonight.
6. He has just called the gas company.
7. He has already had a cup of coffee.
8. Have you ever done this before?
9. I have always wanted to go to Las Vegas.
10. She has met the Prime Minister.
11. I have already finished dinner.
12. They have already said they will go.
13. She has been here for a half an hour.
14. I have read this book before.
15. She has tried to finish her soup, but she's full.

2.

1. Yes, I have drunk Chinese beer a few times/many times.
   No, I have never drunk Chinese beer.
2. Yes, I have flown across the equator a few times/many times.
   No, I have never flown across the equator.
3. Yes, I have been to Australia a few times/many times.
   No, I have never been to Australia.
4. Yes, I have seen the Empire State Building a few times/many times.
   No, I have never seen the Empire State Building.
5. Yes, I have been really hungry a few times/many times.
   No, I have never been really hungry.

3.

1. Have you been to lunch yet?
2. Is Mr. Smith in his office? No, he has gone to the bank.
3. He has never been to our home.
4. Has David gone home yet or is he still here?
5. Has Sarah ever been/gone abroad?

Unit 23

1.

Ann: Have you ever tried caviar?
Bob: No, I have never tried caviar but I tried sushi once.
Ann: When did you try sushi?
Bob: I tried it last year.
Ann: What did you think of it?
Bob: I thought it was great.

Cathy: How many times have you visited your parents this year?
Dave: I have visited them lots of times.
Cathy: When did you last visit them?
Dave: I visited them two months ago.
Cathy: How were they?
Dave: They were well, thanks.

Ella: Have you read his new novel?
Fred: No, I haven't read it yet, but I read his last one.
Ella: When did you read it?
Fred: I read it a few years ago.
Ella: Did you like his last book?
Fred: No, I hated it.

2.

  1.

Ann: Have you ever eaten lobster?
Bob: Yes, I have eaten lobster.
Ann: How many times have you eaten it?
Bob: I have eaten it three times.
Ann: When did you last eat lobster?
Bob: I last ate lobster in 2005.
Ann: Did you like it?
Bob: Yes, I liked it very much.

  2.

Ann: Have you ever seen the Rolling Stones?
Bob: Yes, I have seen the Rolling Stones.
Ann: How many times have you seen them?
Bob: I have seen them three times.
Ann: When did you last see them?
Bob: I last saw them in 2005.
Ann: Did you like them?
Bob: Yes, I liked them very much.

Unit 24

1.

  1.   We have been living here for twelve years.

2. I have been practicing for forty-five minutes.
3. He has been reading that book since last Christmas.
4. They have been playing golf since 8:00.
5. We have been driving for ten hours.
6. She has been working in this factory since 2001.
7. They have been discussing the matter for the last three hours.
8. It has been snowing since last Sunday.
9. You have been making that excuse for twenty years.
10. He has been doing that job since he was a teenager.

2.

1. It has been raining for seven hours.
2. We have been studying English for two years.
3. They have been working since lunch.
4. He just spoke to her ten minutes ago.
5. I have been collecting coins since 1992.
6. You've been writing that letter for three hours.
7. She met him six years ago.
8. I have been reading this chapter since nine o'clock.
9. We have been waiting for ten days.
10. I have been living here since I was a child.

3.

1. We have been studying English for ten years.
2. He has been working in New Orleans since 2004.
3. She has been sitting on that bench for three hours.
4. I have been living in this house since I was a child.
5. He has been cooking for the last 30 minutes.
6. They have been discussing that problem for two days.
7. She has been writing her thesis since 1998.
8. You have been following me for twenty minutes.
9. They have been building that bridge for five years.
10. She has been playing the piano since she was four.

Unit 25

1.

1. I had gone to the health club as soon as I finished work.
2. Everybody had left for the day, so there was nobody at work.
3. Dave had lived in Chicago as a boy, but he moved to New York when he was 18.
4. Barbara immediately phoned her parents, who had reported her missing.
5. Years after it had shut down, the factory burned to the ground.

2.

1. a. Susan remembered everything as if it had happened yesterday.
   b. Susan remembers everything that happened yesterday.
2. a. Why hadn't the government solved the problem before it got so serious?
   b. Why hasn't the government solved the problem by now?

3.   a. They had lived in Oregon for decades before moving to Iowa.
     b. They lived in Oregon for health reasons.
4.   a. He had taken the dog for a walk in the park earlier that morning.
     b. He took the dog for a walk in the park today.
5.   a. I asked if he had talked to his doctor about it when he last saw him.
     b. I asked if he talked to his doctor regularly.

Unit 26

1.

1.   A message was given to me.
2.   Did they plan to stay for the weekend?
3.   He had forgotten to lock the garage door.
4.   He is building a house on a hill above the city.
5.   She may be planning a long vacation abroad.
6.   We hope that you will all come visit us soon.
7.   I have grown these kinds of vegetables for two years.
8.   They had arisen an hour before breakfast.
9.   The cat had torn the newspaper soon after it came.
10. They have taken two trips to the mountains

2.

1.   Have you washed your face yet?
2.   We could go to the mountains later in August.
3.   They had finished their assignment last week.
4.   She could speak Chinese when she was young.
5.   My cousin will send us postcards during his trip.

Unit 27

1.

1.   They looked at the fascinating painting.
     They were fascinated with the painting.
2.   She talked about a frightening movie.
     She was frightened by the movie.
3.   He talked about his irritating brother.
     He is irritated by his brother.
4.   I listened to the moving speech.
     I was moved by the speech.
5.   We had a satisfying meal.
     We were satisfied with the meal.

2.

1.   His talent was so amazing that people came from far away to hear him play.
2.   Did you watch that interesting history show on TV last night?
3.   I was surprised to see how popular American music is around the world.
4.   He filled the washing machine with his clothes.
5.   The astonished reporter was left speechless by the actor's remarks.

Unit 28

1.

1. They used to live in town but now they live in the country.
2. She used to go to church when she was younger.
3. He used to drive a blue car, but now he walks everywhere instead.
4. When I was a child, I used to ride my bike every Saturday.
5. After dinner we waited for the concert to begin.
6. Last Sunday we were lying on a beach.
7. He was living in Europe a few years ago.
8. I used to complain whenever my mother cooked squash for lunch.
9. While I was driving, my cell phone rang.
10. My boss used to yell at me every day, but she stopped last year.

2.

1. I used to vote Republican but now I'm a Democrat.
2. He was telling me his life story when the doorbell rang.
3. I used to like him when we were in school together.
4. While I was waiting, I reread her letter.
5. My mother used to read to us every night when we were children.

3.

1. I used to be a nurse but now I'm a doctor.
2. While we were playing tennis, it started to snow.
3. When the prisoner escaped, the guards were sleeping.
4. We used to go to the beach every day when we were in Florida.
5. Before I went to college I used to hate studying.

Unit 29

1.

1. She will see them next week when she goes home.
2. He will talk to them before he leaves town,
3. I will call you as soon as I have any more news.
4. If I see your sister, I will tell her to call you.
5. She will give us the money when she gets her paycheck.
6. I will finish the cleaning if you watch the kids.
7. Our boss will give us a new assignment after we finish this one.
8. The law probably won't pass until after Congress resumes their session.
9. By the time you read this, I will have left.
10. If you tell me the truth, I will not get angry.

2.

1. I will talk to you before you have your interview.
2. We will write to you as soon as we hear from the manufacturers.
3. As soon as John arrives, he will call you.
4. I will take a photo of the snow before it disappears.
5. When I see Rose next week, I will give her your message.

3.

1. If you visit your grandfather, you will make him very happy.
2. We will have a big meal before you leave.
3. Everything will be ready when the guests arrive.
4. I will give her a call before I forget.
5. We will leave as soon as you are ready.
6. We will not have a picnic if it rains.
7. I will tell you when I know the answer.
8. We will go straight to the beach as soon as we arrive.
9. I will buy the car if it is cheap enough.
10. I will be glad when the exams are over.

Unit 30

1.

1. The principal is suggesting that the new teacher teach solid geometry.
2. The rules require that everyone leave their weapons outside the building.
3. She recommends that you be prepared for anything.
4. He asked that she drive slower through this neighborhood.
5. She insisted that the entire project be completed on schedule.

2.

1. He's the head honcho, as it were.
2. Far be it from me to tell you how to run your business.
3. Suffice it to say that the wedding was fantastic.
4. I know you don't want to go. Be that as it may, however, you have no choice.
5. Come what may, I won't miss the funeral.

Unit 31

1.

1. If I lived by the sea, I would learn to swim.
2. If I won the lottery, I would quit my job.
3. If I had daughters, I would name them after my aunts.
4. If he thought about it, he would understand the joke.
5. If I were you, I would go to college
6. I would not believe him if I were you.
7. If we lived near the mountains, we would hike every day.
8. If she had more time, she would do it for you.

2.

1. If I went to Paris, I would visit your sister.
2. If I were young, I would run the Boston Marathon.
3. If I were you, I would wear that red dress.
4. If I had a car, I would drive to Mexico.
5. If I needed a new radio, I would buy a Sony.
6. If I were as pretty as my sister, I would be very happy.
7. If I had a beach house, I would go to the ocean every week.
8. If he asked her to marry him, she would say yes.

9. If she earned more money, they would go on vacation.
10. If you liked fish, we would go to that restaurant.

3.

1. If I were thinner, I would wear that dress.
    Even if I were thinner, I wouldn't wear that dress.
2. If I had $20,000, I would buy a new car.
    Even if I had $20,000, I wouldn't buy a new car.
3. If I lived in Manhattan, I would go to the theater every week.
    Even if I lived in Manhattan, I wouldn't go to the theater every week.
4. If I spoke German, I would live in Austria.
    Even if I spoke German, I wouldn't live in Austria.
5. If I needed a new computer, I would choose a laptop.
    Even if I needed a new computer, I wouldn't choose a laptop.

Unit 32

1.

1. If I had known that, I would have gone with you.
2. If she had not gotten that job, she would have gone bankrupt.
3. If you had bought the car last month, you would/could have saved a lot of money.
4. If the team had won, we would have gone to the finals.
5. If the van was/were larger, we could/would have taken more people with us.

2.

1. If I had worked hard at school, I would have passed my exams.
2. If he had lived near the ocean, he would have learned to swim when he was a boy.
3. If I had trained, I would have run the marathon.
4. If my parents had had a car, I would have learned to drive.
5. If she had found him, she would have been happy.
6. If the shirts had been made of cotton, I would have bought one.
7. If Mary had tried, she would have beaten John.
8. If Lucy hadn't gotten up late, she wouldn't have missed her flight.
9. If I hadn't lost my temper, I wouldn't have lost my job.
10. If he hadn't fumbled the ball, the other team wouldn't have scored a goal.

3.

1. If I had read the report, I would have understood the situation.
    If I hadn't read the report, I wouldn't have understood the situation.
2. If I had had the money I would have bought a suit.
    If I hadn't had the money, I wouldn't have bought a suit.
3. If I had needed a secretary, I would have hired you.
    If I hadn't needed a secretary, I wouldn't have hired you.
4. If I had known you were making dinner, I would have come home.
    If I hadn't known you were making dinner, I wouldn't have come home.
5. If I had thought about the problem, I would have made the right decision.
    If I hadn't thought about the problem, I wouldn't have made the right decision.

Unit 33

1.

1. I wish we were happier.
2. I wish my office was/were closer to my house.
3. I wish you would say something—your silence is killing me.
4. She wishes she had become a novelist.
5. I wish I had tried harder in school.

2.

1. I wish I earned a lot of money.
2. I wish I were/was as tall as my sister.
3. I wish I owned a good tennis racket.
4. I wish I had a car.
5. I wish I were/was you.
6. I wish I could swim.
7. I wish I had a house in the country.
8. I wish I could afford a new coat.
9. I wish I were/was 20 years old.
10. I wish I were/was going with you.

3.

1. I wish I had won the cup.
2. I wish I had caught the last train.
3. I wish I had run the marathon.
4. I wish I had read books when I was a child.
5. I wish I had learned to swim when I was a boy.
6. I wish I had bought some presents.
7. I wish I hadn't lost his address.
8. I wish I hadn't gotten up late this morning.
9. I wish I hadn't lost my temper.
10. I wish I hadn't crashed my dad's car.

Unit 34

1.

1. The votes were recounted three times.
2. This film has been seen by millions of people.
3. Tons of cards will be sold this Christmas.
4. A thousand houses are sold every year.
5. The painting had been sold by the time I arrived.
6. A new bridge is being built across the river.
7. I was sent this letter ten days ago.
8. This knife is used to chop vegetables.
9. She was given a diamond ring for her birthday.
10. These little holes were made by moths.

2.

1. Once the jar has been opened, it should be refrigerated.
2. By the time I got up, the dishes had been washed.
3. These houses are going to be knocked down and the road is going to be widened.
4. Your sheets will be changed and your room will be cleaned once a week.
5. He had been hit over the head and his wallet had been stolen.

Unit 35

1.

1. When do we need to leave?
2. How many bananas did you eat today?
3. Have you ever visited Greece?
4. Would you like to have some more ice cream?
5. Was it difficult to turn down the job?
6. When do you think we will get there?
7. Who told you the secret?
8. Where did/have you put the keys?
9. How are you feeling?
10. Can we have some ice cream?

2.

1. Have you tried her pie yet?
2. Did you hear what I said?
3. How old are you?
4. To whom are you speaking?
5. What have you done?

Unit 36

1.

1. He said to her that he was sorry.
2. He said that he was sorry.
3. He told her he was sorry.
4. "I'm going to the concert," Peter said.
5. Judy told her mother that she had bought a new dress the day before.
6. Wendy said to me, "I'll be going to the store again tomorrow."
7. Wendy told me that she would be going to the store the next day as well.
8. Peter said that he was going to the concert.

2.

1. Tim told Jenny that he was in London.
2. Sarah told Alice that she would be in New York the next day.
3. Max told Harry that he had a pain in his leg.
4. Her brother told Elizabeth that David worked for Sony.
5. My mother told me that my sister was ill.
6. Jane told Tom that it had been raining earlier.
7. Mr. and Mrs. Wilson said that they had been waiting for two hours.
8. The twins told their teacher that they didn't want to be in the same class.

9. My father told me that his company was losing money.
10. Peter told Laura that the weather had been awful the day before.

3.

1. My mother said to me, "I have been worried for several months."
2. Elizabeth's brother said to her, "I got married two weeks ago."
3. Tim said to Jenny, "I am in love with you."
4. Mr. and Mrs. Wilson said to me, "You can stay with us."
5. Peter said to Laura, "I have lost my job."
6. My brother said to me, "I will be back next week."
7. Sarah said to Alan, "Your wife has a problem."
8. Jane said to Tom, "There is a man here to see you."
9. Max said to Harry, "The police want to speak to us."
10. The twins said to their teacher, "We are ill."

Unit 37

1.

1. Jenny asked where Alice was.
2. Peter asked if I had ever read *Hamlet*.
3. Helen asked Max what he would do.
4. David's brother asked which company David worked for.
5. My mother asked me if I would be home soon.
6. John asked George who lived there.
7. They asked how long I/we had been waiting.
8. The twins asked the teacher if they would be in the same class.
9. My father asked me why I had told her a lie.
10. Paul asked Laura if the hotel was good.

2.

1. "Where is your house, Daniel?" James asked. *or*
    "Daniel, where is your house?" James asked. *or*
    "Where is your house?" James asked Daniel.
2. "Have you ever heard a Beethoven sonata?" Carl asked.
3. "What will you say to your mother, Mark?" Emma asked. *or*
    "What will you say to your mother?" Emma asked Mark. *or*
    "Mark, what will you say to your mother?" Emma asked.
4. "Which dessert would you like, Bob?" his sister asked. *or*
    "Bob, which dessert would you like?" his sister asked. *or*
    "Which dessert would you like?" Bob's sister asked him.
5. "Will you be late?" my father asked me.
6. "Which days do you work, Mrs. Gray?" Barry asked. *or*
    "Mrs. Gray, which days do you work?" Barry asked. *or*
    "Which days do you work," Barry asked Mrs. Gray.
7. "Are you thirsty?" Mr. Johnson asked. *or*
    "Are you thirsty," Mr. Johnson asked me.

8. "Will you wait for us?" the brothers asked their mother. *or*
   "Will you wait for us, Mother?" the brothers asked. *or*
   "Mother, will you wait for us?" the brothers asked.
9. "Why won't you help me?" my sister asked me.
10. "Was the party last night good?" Matthew asked Rachel. *or*
    "Was the party last night good, Rachel?" Matthew asked. *or*
    "Rachel, was the party last night good?" Matthew asked.

Unit 38

1.

1. Don't say a word!
2. Don't do it!
3. She told him to sit down.
4. They told us to go home.
5. He asked me please not to come in.
6. She told him not to say a word.
7. They told us not to do that.
8. Close the door, please. *or*
   Please close the door.
9. Would you answer the phone, please? *or*
   Would you please answer the phone?
10. She told him to close the door.
11. He asked me to please answer the phone.
12. Please don't see her again.
13. She asked if I could fill out the forms for her.
14. Please don't hurt him! *or*
    Don't hurt him, please!
15. Buy me a ticket.

2.

1. Robert told Alice to go away.
2. The teacher told the children to stand up.
3. Maria told Paul not to open the window.
4. Her mother asked/begged Ann to come back home.
5. His aunt asked Peter to speak to his mother.
6. John told David not to let her do it.
7. His sister asked Ian to give her a call.
8. My uncle told me not to spend all my money.
9. Judy asked Carol to help.
10. Their father told the girls not to let anybody into the house.

3.

1. "Don't disturb me, Paul," Maria said. *or*
   "Paul, don't disturb me," Maria said.
2. "Don't leave the house, children," their uncle said. *or*
   "Children, don't leave the house," their uncle said.
3. "Would you answer the phone while I am out, please?" Robert asked.

4. "Don't invest in the scheme, David," John said. *or*
   "David, don't invest in the scheme," John said.
5. "Don't stay out late, girls," their father said. *or*
   "Girls, don't stay out late," their father said.
6. "Would you buy me some milk on your way home please, Peter?" his mother asked. *or*
   "Peter, would you please buy me some milk on your way home?" his mother asked. *or*
   "Peter, would you buy me some milk on your way home, please?" his mother asked.
7. "Please don't leave, Jane," her aunt said/begged. *or*
   "Jane, please don't leave," her aunt said/begged.
8. "Would you be my bridesmaid please, Carol?" Judy asked. *or*
   "Carol, would you be my bridesmaid?" Judy asked.
9. "Be quiet, children!" the teacher said. *or*
   "Children, be quiet!" the teacher said.
10. "Would you give me a lift to work please, Ian?" his sister asked. *or*
    "Ian, would you please give me a lift to work?" his sister asked. *or*
    "Ian, would you give me a lift to work, please?" his sister asked.

Unit 39

1. I hear she might come home tomorrow.
2. She wants to know what you thought of the play.
3. He saw the bug crawl up the wall and jumped up to kill it.
4. Do you think we should wait, or should we go on without him?
5. Do you speak Italian?
6. I would like to learn Italian.
7. You can't make me like broccoli.
8. Is she in? Will you have her call me when she does get in?
9. I need to take a quick shower before we leave.
10. They made him promise to come home before midnight.

Unit 40

1.

1. I am waiting to <u>set up</u> the projector.
2. We <u>settled in</u> for the night.
3. She decided to <u>call in</u>.
4. The dog barked at me until the owner <u>called</u> it <u>off</u>.
5. I hope I can <u>get</u> my point <u>across</u>.
6. The people were just <u>going about</u> their business.
7. When I whistled, the horse's ears <u>perked up</u>.
8. He <u>backed away</u> from the edge of the cliff.
9. What subject are you going to <u>take up</u> in college?
10. <u>Hold on</u>, I'm coming!

2.

1.	transitive	6.	transitive
2.	intransitive	7.	intransitive
3.	intransitive	8.	transitive
4.	transitive	9.	transitive
5.	transitive	10.	intransitive

Unit 41

1.

1. He bought a camera <u>so as to</u> / <u>in order to</u> / <u>to</u> take photos of his dogs.
2. She went to college <u>so as to</u> / <u>in order to</u> / <u>to</u> get a better job.
3. Cyclists should wear bright clothes <u>so as to</u> / <u>in order to</u> / <u>to</u> make them more visible.
4. I go to the gym every day <u>so as to</u> / <u>in order to</u> / <u>to</u> get fit.
5. My parents came here by bus <u>so as to</u> / <u>in order to</u> / <u>to</u> save money.
6. I went to the optometrists <u>so as to</u> / <u>in order to</u> / <u>to</u> have my eyes tested.
7. He went into the house <u>so as to</u> / <u>in order to</u> / <u>to</u> wash his hands.
8. She has gone upstairs <u>so as to</u> / <u>in order to</u> / <u>to</u> rest.

2.

1. He wants to buy a boat so that he can go sailing every weekend.
2. She wants to stop working so that she can spend more time with her children.
3. Athletes train every day so that they can keep fit.
4. I moved to the country so that I could keep horses.
5. She studied hard so that she could impress her professors.

Unit 42

1.

1. The lawyer who/that was in charge of our case met us at the courthouse.
2. The sisters, who went to school with my mother, arrived last night.
3. The man who/whom/that you met yesterday is giving a speech here tonight.
4. My grandparents, who/whom I never knew, lived in Kansas.
5. Norman, with whom I had lunch, is the man in the blue sweater.
6. Those are my daughter's teachers, for whom I have the greatest respect.
7. The blue whale, which is the largest creature that has ever lived, is an endangered species.
8. That is the table that my grandfather made.
9. I tried to learn a lot about the country that I was going to visit.
10. Max is the man who/that caught the thief.

2.

1. The first singer, who lived in Chicago, was the best performer.
2. The defendants, who worked with my brother, were found guilty.
3. Maria, who/whom you have already met, is my best pupil.
4. My favorite painting, which I bought in Spain, is that one.
5. The cheetah, which is the fastest land animal, is a member of the cat family.

Unit 43

1.

1. Do you know which house is his?
2. We visited the mountains, where my uncle has a house.
3. That is why you are never supposed to walk alone at night.
4. The Metropolitan Opera, where Pavarotti gave his last opera performance, is in New York City.
5. That woman, whose husband is the owner of the bank, shops on Rodeo Drive.

2.

1. During the year when he was in the Navy, he was injured.
2. He is the reason why I'm late.
3. The summer when I went abroad was the best summer of my life.
4. That was the night when their house burned down.
5. No one knew the reason why she left.

Unit 44

1.

1. Arthur isn't very busy, is he?
2. It isn't working, is it?
3. Jennifer teaches your son, doesn't she?
4. The news is very depressing, isn't it?
5. Bob doesn't like me very much, does he?
6. Alice and Dave had seen the movie before, hadn't they?
7. I'm older than your sister, aren't I?
8. You can play the piano, can't you?
9. His wife will be with him, won't she?
10. Your son has finished his exams now, hasn't he?
11. You didn't offer her the job, did you?
12. They drove here, didn't they?
13. We loved the play, didn't we?
14. It doesn't worry us, does it?
15. It's cooler on the beach, isn't it?

2.

1. Elizabeth doesn't work here, does she?
2. Charles knows her, doesn't he?
3. I'm taller than your brother, aren't I?
4. It doesn't open until nine o'clock, does it?
5. It isn't snowing, is it?
6. Mary and Jack wouldn't like it here, would they?
7. Christine isn't happy, is she?
8. I'm talking too much, aren't I?
9. Your brother will be at the party, won't he?
10. The weather's awful at the moment, isn't it?
11. They arrived here last week, didn't they?
12. It's cold in here, isn't it?
13. They had met before, hadn't they?
14. Your daughter has learned how to swim, hasn't she?
15. We enjoyed the meal last night, didn't we?

Unit 45

1.

1. There is a new student in the class.
2. There are some flies in the kitchen.

3. It is a good thing that you didn't get hurt.
4. It is three miles to the next gas station.
5. There are not a lot of cherries left on the tree.
6. It will be exciting when he finally gets here.
7. Is there a grocery store nearby?
8. Will there be an intermission during the play tonight?
9. There was a huge flood in Bangladesh yesterday.
10. There are ten minutes left before the end of the class.

2.

1. There are about 300 million people living in the U.S.
2. It will be raining by the time we get there—look at those thunderclouds!
3. There could be some strong winds tonight if the storm blows in.
4. It could be that she left already and that's why the door is locked.
5. Is there some pizza left in the refrigerator?
6. It is snowing in the mountains right now.
7. There is no smoke without fire.
8. Are there any good restaurants near here?
9. There isn't any hope of a snowy Christmas this year because it has been so warm.
10. It was almost midnight before she arrived.

Unit 46

1.

1. It is the doctor who ~~he~~ often suggests a new brand of drug.
2. Tonsillitis is one condition that ~~it~~ is curable.
3. Everyone needs friends who ~~they~~ are loyal.
4. The window, which is now clean, ~~it~~ reflects the sun.
5. Places where it is quiet and peaceful ~~they~~ are rare.
6. That winter especially was the time when he was working hard ~~then~~.
7. Tom, my brother, ~~he~~ never misses the basketball games on TV.
8. I know the lady whose dog ~~it~~ is wearing a jacket.
9. He believes that you are what ~~that~~ you eat.
10. Sharon didn't say why the package ~~it~~ should not be opened.

2.

1. (correct)   4. which
2. (correct)   5. (correct)
3. who/whom/that

Unit 47

1.

1. No, I have my car serviced at a garage.
2. No, I have my nails done at a salon.
3. No, she has her hair dyed at the hairdresser's.
4. No, I had my house painted by house painters.
5. No, he had it designed by a gardener.

2.

1. She should have the curtains cleaned.
2. She should have the lock on the front gate fixed.
3. She should have her nails done.
4. She should have the cars serviced.
5. She should have the outside of the house painted.
6. She should have the basement window replaced.
7. She should have her grass cut.
8. She should have the bathroom wallpaper fixed.
9. She should have the chimneys cleaned.
10. She should have the basement decorated.

Unit 48

1.

1. You must sweep the floors before your friends can come over. *or*
    You have to sweep the floors before your friends can come over.
2. She does not have to make a cake.
3. You don't have to be here until 10:00.
4. I had to finish the paper before I went home.
5. If she left the company, we would have to hire a replacement.
6. You must be on time: you cannot be late. *or*
    You have to be on time: you cannot be late.
7. If you want to pass your exams, you must work harder. *or*
    If you want to pass your exams, you have to work harder.
8. I must try to visit my parents more often. *or*
    I have to try to visit my parents more often.
9. You don't have to have a passport to leave the state.
10. You usually have to wait for hours before someone can see you.

2.

1. a. You must wear a swimsuit.
    b. You must not leave trash on the beach.
    c. You must not swim when the sea is rough.
2. a. You must not touch the food with your bare hands.
    b. You must wear plastic gloves.
    c. You don't have to work with any piece of equipment you are not comfortable using.
3. a. You must not be rude.
    b. You must be helpful.
    c. You don't have to say sir or madam, though the customer may think it is nice.
4. a. You must wear shoes.
    b. You don't have to wear a jacket, but we would prefer it.
    c. You must not bring pets into the restaurant.
5. a. You must eat vegetables.
    b. You don't have to eat mushrooms if you don't want to.
    c. You must not eat meat.

Unit 49

1.

Bill: Dan, would you bring us a hammer?

Dan: I'll take it up when I go up the ladder.

Tom: When will you come up here?

Dan: As soon as I'm done unloading the roofing materials. Do you need me to take/bring anything else?

Tom: If you'd bring me some water, that would be great.

Bill: And if you could take this crowbar and put it back in the truck, I'd appreciate it.

Dan: I'll bring you the hammer and some water and then take the crowbar back to the truck, then.

2.

1.	coming	6.	go/come
2.	go/come	7.	coming
3.	going	8.	come
4.	go/come	9.	come/go
5.	going	10.	going

Unit 50

1.

1. I am not used to wearing heels.
2. She is not used to working in an office.
3. They are not used to American money.
4. I am used to speaking English.
5. I can't get used to getting up early. *or*
   I am not used to getting up early.

2.

1.	auxiliary	4.	auxiliary
2.	adjective	5.	auxiliary, adjective
3.	adjective		

Index

a, an, 13–15
abstract nouns, 16
adjectives, 12, 32–35, 36–38, 44–46, 48–50, 50–53, 123–125
 comparative, 32–35
 hyphenated, 48–50
 ordering of, 50–53
 proper, 12
 relative, 123–125
 superlatives, 36–38
adverbs, 33, 37, 44–48, 53–54, 59, 132–133
 comparative, 33
 of frequency, 59
 position of, 53–54
 relative, 132–133
 superlative, 37
ago, 69–71
all, 29–31
any, 21–24
apostrophes, 6–10
articles, 13–20
attributives, 51–52
auxiliaries, 55–56, 74–76, 100

be, 74–76
bring, 139–141

capitalization, 10–13
come, 139–141
commands, 109–113
comparatives, 32–35
conditional sentences, 86–93
continuous tenses, 59–62, 69–71, 142–143, 145, 146–147, 148–149
contractions, 6–10
count nouns, 4–6, 24–29

defining clauses, 120–125
definite article, 16–20
direct speech, 101–113
do, 74–76

each, 29–31
enough, 39–41
entire, 29–31
every, 29–31

few, fewer, 27–29
for, 69–71, 118–120
future continuous, 148–149
future perfect tense, 149
future tense, simple, 82–84, 147–148

get (something done), 134–136
go, 139–141

have, 74–76
have (something done), 134–136
have to, 136–139

if-clauses, 86–93
indefinite article, 13–15
indirect speech, 101–113
infinitives, 113–114, 118–120
irregular verbs, 150–152
it-clauses, 129–131

less, 27–29, 32–35
little, 27–29

many, 24–26
more, 32–35
much, 24–26
modal auxiliaries, 55–56
must, 136–139

noncount nouns, 4–6, 24–29
nondefining clauses, 120–125
nouns, 1–6, 8–9, 10–13, 16, 24–29
 abstract, 16
 count, 4–6, 24–29
 noncount, 4–6, 24–29
 plural, 8–9
 proper, 10–13

omission of letters, 6–10

participles, 76–78
passive voice, 97–99
past continuous, 146–147
past participles, 76–78
past perfect tense, 72–73, 147
past tense, simple, 66–68, 72, 145–146
perfect tenses, 62–65, 66–68, 69–71, 72–73,
        82, 144–145, 147, 149
phrasal verbs, 115–117
plurals, 1–6, 8–9
possession, 6–10
present continuous , 59–62, 143–144
present participles, 76–78
present perfect continuous , 69–71, 145
present perfect tense, 62–65, 66–68, 82,
        144–145
present tense, simple, 59–62, 143
pronouns, relative, 132–133
proper adjectives, 12
proper nouns, 10–13

questions, 100–101, 106–109, 125–128
    reported, 106–109
    tag, 125–128

relative adjectives, 123–125
relative adverbs, 132–133
relative clauses, 120–125, 132–133
relative pronouns, 132–133
reported commands, 109–113

reported questions, 106–109
reported statements, 101–105

say, 103–105
simple future tense, 82–84, 147–148
simple past tense, 66–68, 72, 145–146
simple present tense, 59–62, 143
since, 69–71
so, 42–44
some, 21–24
subjunctive, 84–86, 87, 91, 93
such, 42–44
superlatives, 36–38
tag questions, 125–128
take, 139–141

tell, 101–105
the, 16–20
there-clauses, 129–131
third-person singular, 57–58
too, 39–41

used to (adjective), 141–142
used to (auxiliary), 78–81

when, 79–80, 82
whole, 29–31
wh- questions, 100–101
wish, 93–96

yes/no questions, 100–101

Bob Marsden taught English for several years in France, Sweden, and Switzerland before becoming director of studies at a language school in England. He then worked for the BBC World Service as a producer of programs for teaching English as a second language, first by radio, then by television and video. For the past ten years he has been a full-time EFL writer, producing a variety of materials for learning English by self-study, including textbooks, partworks, CDs, and DVDs.